PRESENTING IN ENGLISH

how to give successful presentations

Mark Powell

THOMSON

HEINLE

Australia Canada Mexico Singapore Spain United Kingdom United States

Presenting in English
How to Give Successful Presentations
Mark Powell

Publisher/Global ELT: *Christopher Wenger*
Executive Marketing Manager, Global ELT/ESL: *Amy Mabley*

Printed in Croatia by Zrinski d.d.
1 2 3 4 5 6 7 8 9 10   06 05 04 03 02

For more information contact Heinle, 25 Thomson Place, Boston, MA 02210 USA,
or you can visit our Internet site at http://www.heinle.com

For permission to use material from this text or product contact us:
Tel   1-800-730-2214
Fax   1-800-730-2215
Web   www.thomsonrights.com

ISBN: 1 899396 30 6

Cassette Tape
A cassette tape accompanies this book. All material recorded on the cassette is clearly marked.
The cassette is available in two editions, one with British pronunciation and one with American
pronunciation.

British version	**ISBN 1 89396 50 0**
English version	**ISBN 1 899396 75 6**

The Author
Mark Powell has taught English in the UK and throughout Europe. He has extensive experience
teaching business English and is a well-known teacher trainer in this field. He is the author of the
business English course **Business Matters**.

Acknowledgements
Cover design by Anna Macleod
Cover photography courtesy of Richard Bryant and Arcaid
Illustrations by Jonathan Marks
Graphs on pages 26 and 27 courtesy of The European

Section 4   Basic Techniques

Section 5   Further Techniques

Section 6   Key Language

Section 7   Handling Questions

Answer Key

Using this Book

1. What makes a good presentation?

Without exception, all good presenters have one thing in common, enthusiasm, both for their subject and for the business of presenting it. Enthusiasm is infectious. Audiences can't help but be affected by it. And the best public speakers always make what they say sound as if it really matters. They know that if it matters to them, it will matter to their audience.

Many things contribute to the success of a presentation – new and unusual content, a clear structure, a good sense of timing, imaginative use of visual aids, the ability to make people laugh . . . and think. But above and beyond all of these is enthusiasm. What kind of language and what kind of techniques will best show your enthusiasm for your subject?

2. How is this book different?

Based on the latest research into business communications, **Presenting in English** analyzes what makes a speaker sound dynamic and enthusiastic. It identifies the key skills employed by all effective presenters. The basics of introducing your topic, structuring your talk and referring to visual aids are dealt with in Sections 1 and 2. The remainder of the book focuses on:

Voice and Delivery   As a presenter, the ability to pace your speech and use your voice to create impact is the single most important skill you need. You will be more effective if you are in control of your voice by your use of stress, pausing, intonation, volume, and silence.

Content Language   You can't give a good presentation unless you have something to say. Being confident about your content is crucial. **Presenting in English** helps you to identify and organize all the key words and phrases you are likely to need and teaches you how to make simple visuals work for you.

Rhetorical Technique   Once you are in charge of both your voice and your content you can start to think about how best to present your subject. Sections 4 and 5 teach you the techniques successful speakers use automatically. Choose the techniques that suit you best and work on perfecting them.

Question Handling   Perhaps the most unpredictable part of a presentation is the question session. This may be after your talk or you may invite questions during it. Section 7 systematically teaches you how to field different types of question and deal effectively with the subjects your audience may raise.

3. Using this book

In class   If you are an inexperienced presenter, it is probably best to work through the course section by section, making sure you do all the presentations before you move on. Pay special attention to the basic skills in Sections 1 – 3.

If you give presentations in English regularly and want to improve your style, go through the contents list with your teacher first and decide which areas to concentrate on.

When you give short presentations in class, take the time to prepare your notes thoroughly with any visuals you might need. Don't be afraid to read out some of the most important or complicated parts of your talk. As long as you read them well and keep good eye contact with your audience, this can be very effective.

At home If you are working alone, use the cassette as much as possible, as it will give you the vital listening input you need. Play it again at home or while driving.

If you can, get a friend or colleague to listen to you giving short presentations yourself. Try recording some of your talks and compare yourself with the speakers on the course cassette.

A lot of the presentation extracts in the course book contain phrases and expressions which you could use directly yourself. Sometimes whole sentences and paragraphs could be used with only small changes. Make a habit of noting these down for future use.

Try to study regularly if you can. Most of the units in **Presenting in English** are only one or two pages long. Try to cover three or four units a week. Even doing two units a week is better than doing nothing for months and then going into a panic the day before you have to give your presentation! Gradually build up your competence and confidence.

4. Using the cassettes

Many of the input tasks in **Presenting in English** consist of short presentation extracts which are recorded on cassette. Exercises which are on tape are marked like this `cass` .

When you have completed an input task, listen to the cassette to check your answers before looking in the key at the back of the book. This provides you with useful listening practice and a model of good delivery as well as the correct answers.

5. How to become a good presenter

1. LEAVE NOTHING TO CHANCE

Check everything before you are due to speak – room, seating, visibility, acoustics and equipment.

2. KNOW EXACTLY HOW TO START

Plan the first minute of your presentation down to the last detail. Try to memorize your opening words. This will help you to sound confident and in control.

3. GET STRAIGHT TO THE POINT

Don't waste time on long boring introductions. Try to make at least one powerful statement in the first two minutes.

4. TALK *TO* YOUR AUDIENCE

Many of the best presentations sound more like conversations. So, keep referring back to your audience, ask them questions, respond to their reactions.

5. KNOW WHAT WORKS

Certain things are always popular with an audience: personal experiences, stories with a message, dramatic comparisons, amazing facts they didn't know. Use them to the full.

6. BE CONCISE

Keep your sentences short and simple. Use deliberate pauses to punctuate your speech.

7. SPEAK NATURALLY

Don't be afraid to hesitate when you speak, but make sure you pause in the right places. Remember, you are not an actor trying to remember lines. A certain amount of hesitation is actually quite natural.

8. KNOW YOUR AUDIENCE

Speak for your audience, not yourself. Take every opportunity to show how much common ground you share with them. Address *their* goals, *their* needs, *their* concerns.

9. TREAT YOUR AUDIENCE AS EQUALS

Never talk down (or up) to your audience. Treat them as equals, no matter who they are.

10. BE YOURSELF

As far as possible, speak to five hundred people in much the same way you would speak to five. You will obviously need to project yourself more, but your personality shouldn't change.

11. TAKE YOUR TIME

Whenever you make a really important point, pause and let the full significance of what you have said sink in . . . before you move on.

12. DON'T MAKE A SPECIAL EFFORT TO BE FUNNY

If you make a joke, don't stop and wait for laughs. Keep going and let the laughter (if it comes) interrupt you.

13. LET YOUR VISUALS SPEAK FOR THEMSELVES

Good visuals are just that – visual. Don't put boring tables of figures and long lines of text on the overhead and read them out. Stick to the main points. Experiment with three-dimensional charts, cartoons, interesting typefaces – anything to catch your audience's attention.

14. NEVER COMPETE WITH YOUR VISUALS

When showing a visual, keep quiet and give people time to take it in. Then make brief comments only. Point to the relevant parts of the visual as you speak. If you want to say more, switch off your projector to do so.

15. DEVELOP YOUR OWN STYLE

Learn from other public speakers, but don't try to copy them. Be comfortable with your own abilities. Don't do anything that feels unnatural for you, just because it works for someone else.

16. ENJOY THE EXPERIENCE

The secret of being an excellent speaker is to enjoy the experience of speaking – try to enjoy the experience!

17. WELCOME QUESTIONS FROM YOUR AUDIENCE

When members of your audience ask you a question, it is usually because they have a genuine interest in what you are saying and want to know more. Treat questions as an opportunity to get your message across better.

18. FINISH STRONGLY

When you are ready to finish your presentation, slow down, and lower your voice. Look at the audience and deliver your final words slowly and clearly. Pause, let your words hang in the air a moment longer, smile, say *Thank you* and then sit down.

Getting Started

How to make an immediate impact on your audience

"Could you talk amongst yourselves . . . . it looks as if I've left my notes in my hotel."

Introductions

> How you begin your presentation depends on how formal the situation is. Most audiences prefer a relatively informal approach.

TASK 1

Below you will find two alternative ways of introducing yourself and the subject of your presentation – one fairly formal, the other more friendly. At each stage choose the expression you would feel more comfortable using and highlight it.

FAIRLY FORMAL	MORE FRIENDLY
Erm, perhaps we should begin.	OK, let's get started.
Good morning, ladies and gentlemen.	Morning, everyone.
On behalf of . . . , may I welcome you to . . .	Thanks for coming.
My name's . . .	I'm . . .
For those of you who don't know me already,	As you know, . . .
I'm responsible for . . .	I'm in charge of . . .
This morning I'd like to . . .	What I want to do this morning is . . .
discuss . . .	talk to you about . . .
report on . . .	tell you about . . .
and present . . .	and show you . . .
If you have any questions you'd like to ask, I'll be happy to answer them. or Perhaps we can leave any questions you may have until the end of the presentation.	Feel free to ask any questions you like as we go along. And don't worry, there'll be plenty of time left over for questions at the end.

How happy would you be taking questions a) during your presentation b) at the end?

TASK 2

Now put together an introduction of your own using some of the expressions you chose above. Remember how important it is to be totally confident about this part of your presentation.

> Don't waste a lot of time at the beginning of your presentation introducing yourself, your company and the subject of your talk. Get on with it!

Stating Your Purpose 1

It is essential to state the purpose of your presentation near the beginning.
To do this clearly and effectively you need a few simple presentation verbs:
take a look at, report on, give an overview of etc.

`cass` **TASK**

Below you will find a number of ways of stating the purpose of your presentation.
Complete them using the words given. Combining the sentences with the number 1 will give
you a complete introduction. Then do the same with those numbered 2 etc.
The cassette provides a good model for you. Use it to check your answers after you have
done the exercise.

OK, let's get started. Good morning, everyone. Thanks for coming. I'm (your name).

This morning I'm going to be:

showing   talking   taking   reporting   telling

1. . . . .   to you about the videophone project.
2. . . . .   you about the collapse of the housing market in the early 90s.
3. . . . .   you how to deal with late payers.
4. . . . .   a look at the recent boom in virtual reality software companies.
5. . . . .   on the results of the market study we carried out in Austria.

. . . so, I'll begin by:

making   outlining   bringing   giving   filling

1. . . . .   you in on the background to the project.
2. . . . .   a few observations about the events leading up to that collapse.
3. . . . .   company policy on bad debt.
4. . . . .   you an overview of the history of VR.
5. . . . .   you up-to-date on the latest findings of the study.

. . . and then I'll go on to:

put   discuss   make   highlight   talk

1. . . . .   what I see as the main advantages of the new system.
2. . . . .   the situation into some kind of perspective.
3. . . . .   you through our basic debt management procedure.
4. . . . .   detailed recommendations regarding our own R&D.
5. . . . .   in more depth the implications of the data in the files in front of you.

Highlight all the verb phrases above, eg. *talking to you about, making a few observations
about*. Notice it is not the verb alone, but the whole phrase you need to learn.

PRESENTATION

Prepare to introduce and state the purpose of a presentation of your own by completing the notes below. Then present your introduction.

Perhaps we should begin.   or   OK, let's get started.
Good morning / afternoon / evening, everyone.

Thanks for coming. I'm . . . . And, as you know, I . . . .
. . . .
. . . .
. . . .

This morning I'm going to be
- talking to you about
- telling you
- showing you
- reporting on
- taking a look at

. . . .
. . . .

So, I'll start off by
- filling you in on the background to
- bringing you up-to-date on
- giving you an overview of
- making a few observations about
- outlining

. . . .
. . . .

And then I'll go on to
- highlight what I see as the main
- put the situation into some kind of perspective
- discuss in more depth the implications of
- talk you through
- make detailed recommendations regarding

. . . .
. . . .

Stating Your Purpose 2

When you give a presentation in English, clarity is very important, particularly if there are non-native speakers in your audience. It often helps if you state your purpose at each stage of your talk as well as at the beginning.

TASK

Cross out the verbs which do not fit in the following presentation extracts. The first one has been done for you as an example.

1. First of all, I'd like to ~~preview~~ / ~~overview~~ / **outline** the main points of my talk.

2. Perhaps I should start off by **pointing / stressing / reminding** that this is just a preliminary report. Nothing has been finalized as yet.

3. But later on I will, in fact, be **putting forward / putting out / putting over** several detailed proposals.

4. One thing I'll be **dealing with / referring / regarding** is the issue of a minimum wage.

5. And I'll also be **asking / raising / putting** the question of privatization.

6. So, what we're really **driving at / aiming at / looking at** are likely developments in the structure of the company over the next five to ten years.

7. If we could just **draw / focus / attract** our attention on the short-term objectives to begin with.

8. The eighteen-month plan, which by now you should've all had time to look at, **outlines / reviews / sets out** in detail our main recommendations.

9. Basically, what we're **suggesting / asking / reviewing** is a complete reorganization of staff and plant.

10. I'd now like to **turn / draw / focus** my attention to some of the difficulties we're likely to face.

11. I'm sure there's no need to **draw out / spell out / think out** what the main problem is going to be.

12. But we do need to seriously **ask / answer / address** the question of how we are going to overcome it.

13. The basic message I'm trying to **get through / get across / get to** here is simple. We can't rely on government support for much longer.

14. Disappointing end-of-year figures **underline / undermine / underestimate** the seriousness of the situation.

15. And the main conclusion we've **thought / got to / come to** is that massive corporate restructuring will be necessary before any privatization can go through.

Effective Openings

Communications experts are all agreed that the first three minutes of a presentation are the most important. They talk about 'hooks' – simple techniques for getting the immediate attention of the audience.
A good start makes you feel more confident. Here's how the experts suggest you 'hook' your audience:

1.   Give them a problem to think about.
2.   Give them some amazing facts.
3.   Give them a story or personal anecdote.

`cass` **TASK**

Look at the presentation openings below and divide them under three headings:

PROBLEMS	AMAZING FACTS	STORIES

What do you think each presentation was about?

1. **Did you know that** Japanese companies spend four times more on entertaining clients in a year than the entire GDP of Bulgaria? 40 billion dollars, **to be precise. You know, that's** twice Colombia's total foreign debt. You could buy General Motors for the same money.

2. **Suppose** your advertising budget was cut by 99% tomorrow. **How would you** go about promoting your product?

3. **According to the latest study,** by 2050 only one in every four people in Western Europe will be going to work. And two will be old age pensioners.

4. **You know,** R&D is 90% luck. **When I think about** creativity, **I'm reminded of** the man who invented the microwave oven. He spent years messing around with radar transmitters, then noticed the chocolate in his pocket was starting to melt!

5. **Statistics show that** in the last ten years more people have legally emigrated to the United States than to the rest of the world put together – about half a million of them a year, **in fact. Now,** over ten years, **that's roughly equivalent to** the population of Greece.

6. **Have you ever wondered why it is that** Americans are easier to sell to than Europeans? And why nine out of ten sales gurus are American? **You have? Well, if I could show you** what stops Europeans buying, **would you be interested?**

7. **I read somewhere the other day that** the world's highest paid executive works for Disney and gets $230 million a year. **Now that's about** $2000 a minute! **That means** he's currently making more money than Volkswagen.

8. **How many people here this morning** hate going to meetings? Just about everybody, **right?** **Well, imagine** a company where there were never any meetings and everything ran smoothly. **Do you think that's possible?**

9. **Have you ever been in the situation where** you've had to negotiate with the Japanese? **I remember when** I was working in Nagoya and everybody had told me the Japanese don't like saying *no*. So in meetings I just kept saying *yeah* to everything. And they hated it. **It turned out** *yeah* sounds like *no* in Japanese!

PRESENTATION

Use the frames below to help you prepare effective openings, using the problem, amazing facts, or story technique. Whatever technique you choose, prepare your opening carefully. You should always know exactly how you are going to start.

PROBLEM TECHNIQUE

1. Suppose . . . .
   How would you . . . . ?
2. Have you ever wondered why it is that . . . .
   . . . . ? You have?
   Well, if I could show you . . . .
   . . . . would you be interested?
3. How many people here this morning / afternoon / evening . . . .
   . . . . ?
   Well, imagine . . . .
   . . . . Do you think that's possible?

AMAZING FACTS TECHNIQUE

1. Did you know that . . . . ?
2. According to the latest study, ...
3. Statistics show that . . . .
4. I read somewhere the other day that . . . .

STORY / ANECDOTE TECHNIQUE

1. You know, ...
   When I think about . . . .
   I'm reminded of . . . .
2. Have you ever been in the situation where . . . . ?
   I remember when . . . .
   It turned out . . . .

Signposting

In a good presentation, what you say – the content – is much more important than anything else. But a clear structure helps. When you move on to your next point or change direction, tell the audience.

You can do this easily and effectively, using simple phrases as 'signposts' to guide the audience through your presentation:

To move on	To go back	To summarize
To expand on	To recap	To turn to
To digress	To conclude	To elaborate on

TASK 1

Choose one of the 'signpost' expressions from the box above for the following situations:

1. When you want to make your next point.　　To . . . .

2. When you want to change direction.　　To . . . .

3. When you want to refer to an earlier point.　　To . . . .

4. When you want to repeat the main points.　　To . . . .

5. When you want to give a wider perspective.　　To . . . .

6. When you want to do a deeper analysis.　　To . . . .

7. When you just want to give the basics.　　To . . . .

8. When you want to depart from your plan.　　To . . . .

9. When you want to finish your talk.　　To . . . .

`cass` ## TASK 2

These nine basic signposts are all you need, but you have to remember them automatically. Listen to your cassette or your teacher. When you hear an instruction, for example, *make your next point,* write the correct phrase:

1. . . . .

2. . . . .

3. . . . .

4. . . . .

5. . . . .

6. . . . .

7. . . . .

8. . . . .

9. . . . .

cass **TASK 3**

Once you know the nine basic signposts, you can build them into the points you make to give direction and coherence to your presentation.

Complete the following signpost phrases and sentences using the notes to help you. Say them first. Then write them down. The first one has been done for you as an example.

1. Moving on / question / the US market,
   Moving on to the question of the US market,

2. Expand / the figures / last year,
   . . . .

3. I'd like / recap / the main points.
   . . . .

4. Let's go back / question / clinical research methods.
   . . . .

5. Digress / a moment, let's consider / alternatives.
   . . . .

6. Going back / a moment / the situation last year,
   . . . .

7. Let's turn now / our targets / the next five years.
   . . . .

8. I'd like / turn now / our projections / year 2005.
   . . . .

9. Go back / the main reason / our collaboration / the Germans,
   . . . .

10. I'd like / expand / that / little, before we move on.
    . . . .

11. Let's go back / a moment / what we were discussing earlier.
    . . . .

12. Let me expand / some / the main points / our proposal.
    . . . .

13. Elaborate / that / little / those of you / aren't familiar / Russian business practices,
    . . . .

14. If I could just move on / some / the problems we face / Central / Latin America,
    . . . .

15. I'd like / conclude / I may / repeating what I said / the beginning / this presentation.
    . . . .

Present the signpost sentences above until you feel comfortable saying them.

Neat, short signposts are more effective than long explanations of the structure of your presentation. Remember, the simplest way to signpost the end of one stage of your presentation and the beginning of the next is to say:
OK. So, ...

Survival Tactics

> Giving a presentation in a foreign language is a challenge. Concentrate too hard on the facts and you make language mistakes. Concentrate too hard on your English and you get your facts wrong.

TASK 1

If you have problems during your presentation, don't panic. Pause. Sort out the problem and continue. Here are the eight most common problems people face. Match what you think with what you say:

WHAT YOU THINK

1. I've got my facts wrong!
2. Too fast! Go back.
3. I've forgotten to say something!
4. Too complicated! Make it simple.

5. I'm talking nonsense.
6. How do you say this in English?
7. Wrong! Try again.
8. I'm running out of time!

WHAT YOU SAY

a. So, let's just recap on that.
b. So, basically, what I'm saying is this . . .
c. Sorry, what I meant is this . . .
d. Sorry, I should just mention one thing.

e. So, just to give you the main points here . . .
f. Sorry, let me rephrase that.
g. Sorry, what's the word / expression?
h. Sorry, perhaps I didn't make that quite clear.

Notice how some of the words are stressed in each phrase. Repeat the phrases until you feel comfortable saying them.

cass TASK 2

Knowing how to get out of difficulty in a presentation is essential. If you learn these expressions by heart, you will be able to do it automatically and, therefore, confidently. Listen to the following problems and use the correct survival phrase.

1. Facts wrong!
2. Too fast!
3. Forgotten something!
4. Too complicated!
5. Talking nonsense!
6. Don't know the English!
7. Sounds wrong!
8. No time!

> Sorry, what . . . . meant . . . . this.
> So, let's . . . . recap . . . . that.
> Sorry, ... should . . . . mention . . . . thing.
> So, basically, ... saying . . . . this.
> Sorry, perhaps . . . . didn't make . . . . clear.
> Sorry, ... word . . . . looking for?
> Sorry, let . . . . rephrase . . . . .
> So, just . . . . give . . . . main . . . . here.

Repeat this activity several times until you can do it automatically.

Exploiting Visuals

How to use visual aids to maximum effect

"I hope you can read this from the back."

Introducing Visuals

Visuals are important in any professional presentation. But when you give a presentation in a foreign language, they are even more important. Visual information is highly memorable and reduces the amount of talking you have to do. Good visuals speak for you.

TASK 1

Divide the visuals below into three groups:

1. GRAPHS _____

2. CHARTS _____

3. DIAGRAMS _____

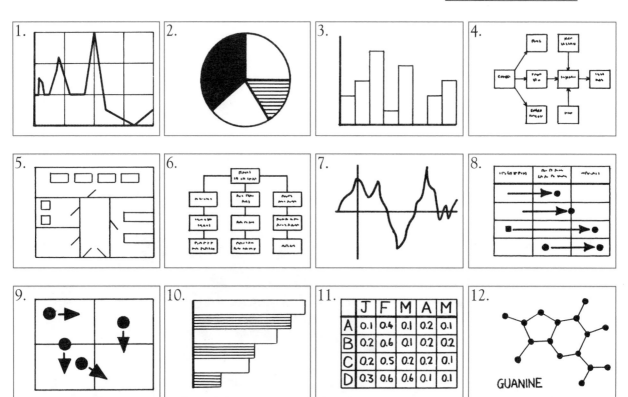

What sort of visuals do you regularly use in your job?

You don't need to know all the names of the different types of visual in order to present them. Simply say:

Have a look at this. or **Take a look at this.**

As you can see, here... and here... .

American English prefers *take* (take a look, take a shower, take a break).

British English prefers *have* (have a look, have a shower, have a break).

cass **TASK 2**

Effective presenters introduce and highlight visual information briefly and clearly. Remember to keep everything simple. Write out the following sentence fragments in the correct order to make complete presentation extracts. The cassette provides a good model for you. Use it to check your answers after you have done the exercise.

EXTRACT 1

see, it's a fairly typical growth

Have a look at

stages of its development. The vertical axis

and the horizontal

this graph. As you can

shows turnover in millions of dollars

curve for a young company in the early

axis represents the years 1990 to 1996

EXTRACT 2

productivity of our European

levels in the Netherlands, shown

looking at very clearly

plants, and gives you some

The graph we're

here, exceed the rest

idea of how far production

demonstrates the comparative

EXTRACT 3

products. Let's take a closer

which shows the current

growth sector

I'd like you

position of six of our leading

movement in the high

to look at this chart,

look for a moment at product

Now underline the most useful expressions used to introduce visuals and highlight key points.

Commenting on Visuals

Visuals help you to give a lot of information in a short space of time. They are really 'quick snapshots' of situations, developments, events and processes which would take a long time to explain fully in words.

Good visuals speak for themselves and require little or no description, but you often need to draw your audience's attention to one or more key points before you discuss them in more detail:

1. Highlights	Which parts of the visual are most significant?
2. Comments	Why?
3. Interpretations	What conclusions can you draw?

TASK 1

These expressions highlight important information in a visual. Complete them using the following words:

on   to   at   out   about

	us to look	1. . . . . . . this part of the graph in more detail.
	us to focus our attention	2. . . . . . . one particularly important feature.
I'd like	you to think	3. . . . . . . the significance of this figure here.
	to point	4. . . . . . . one or two interesting details.
	to draw your attention	5. . . . . . . the upper half of the chart.

TASK 2

These expressions comment on important information in a visual. Complete them using the following words:

If   As   Whatever   Whichever   However

1. . . . . you can see, there are several surprising developments.

2. . . . . you look at it more closely, you'll notice a couple of apparent anomalies.

3. . . . . you try to explain it, this is very bad news.

4. . . . . the reasons for this, the underlying trend is obvious.

5. . . . . way you look at it, these are some of our best results ever.

TASK 3

These expressions interpret important information in a visual. Complete them using the following words:

> lesson   message   significance   conclusions   implications

I'm sure the

1. . . . . to be drawn from this are
2. . . . . to be learned from this is
3. . . . . of this are   clear to all of us.
4. . . . . of this is
5. . . . . here is

Now highlight all the useful expressions, eg. *I'd like us to look at, I'd like us to focus our attention on* etc.

TASK 4

In the box below prepare a visual which is relevant to your work, company or interests. Present it several times, using the suggested expressions to help you.

Introduction and Explanation

Take a look at this / Let's have a look at this / I'd like you to look at this.
Here we can see . . . .
The . . . . . . represents . . . . And the . . . . . . represents . . . .

Highlights and Comments

I'd like us to look at . . . . . . in more detail. As you can see, ...
I'd also like to draw your attention to . . . .
If you look at it more closely, you'll notice . . . .

Interpretations

I'm sure the implications of this / the conclusions to be drawn from this are clear to all of us.

Change and Development 1

> In many professional presentations you need to talk about changes and developments. Usually a visual will explain these for you. But if you do not have a visual to illustrate a particular point, you need the specialized language of change and development.

TASK 1

Here are the most important verbs used to talk about change and development. Complete them by adding the vowels a, e, i, o and u.

1. _ n c r _ _ s _   3. d _ c r _ _ s _   5. s h _ _ t _ p   7. p l _ n g _

2. r _ s _   4. f _ l l   6. t _ k _ _ f f   8. s l _ m p

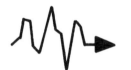  

9. f l _ c t _ _ t _   10. r _ c _ v _ r   12. s t _ b _ l _ z _   14. r _ m _ _ n s t _ _ d y

                  11. p _ c k _ p   13. l _ v _ l _ f f

  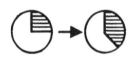 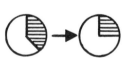

15. p _ _ k   16. h _ t _ l _ w   18. g r _ w   20. s h r _ n k

                17. b _ t t _ m _ _ t   19. _ x p _ n d   21. d _ c l _ n _

TASK 2

Now answer the following questions:

1. Which of these verbs are irregular (eg. rise – rose – risen)?
2. Which can be both a verb and a noun (eg. to rise – a rise)?
3. Which can be changed into a noun (eg. fluctuate – fluctuation)?

Change and Development 2

Sometimes it is not enough to talk about increases and decreases. You may also want to draw your audience's attention to the scale and speed of the change and comment on its significance.

TASK 1

Write the following adjectives in the correct space on the diagram below according to what kind of change they describe:

a(n)	substantial disastrous	rapid moderate	encouraging disappointing	slight steady	spectacular enormous	increase

BIG
1. . . . .
2. . . . .
3. . . . .
4. . . . .
SMALL

FAST
5. . . . .
6. . . . .
SLOW

GOOD
7. . . . .
8. . . . .
9. . . . .
10. . . . .
BAD

Which of the words above mean more or less the same as the following:

a. massive . . . .

b. gradual . . . .

c. significant . . . .

d. tremendous . . . .

TASK 2

Cross out the word which does not fit in the following sentences:

1. Demand increased slightly / steadily / tremendously / disappointingly.

2. Interest rates rose sharply / considerably / keenly / marginally.

3. Profitability slumped moderately / disastrously / suddenly / rapidly.

4. The price of oil fluctuated enormously / wildly / gradually / dramatically.

Now re-write the sentences above using a noun instead of a verb:

1. There was a(n) . . . .
2. There was a(n) . . . .
3. There was a(n) . . . .
4. There was a(n) . . . .

Change and Development 3

Except in complex technical and scientific presentations, you don't usually need to quote precise figures. It is better to include these in a handout or report given out before or after your talk.

It can be helpful, however, when describing very detailed visual aids, to mention *overall* trends and *approximate* figures.

cass TASK 1

Below you will find an extract from a presentation comparing stock market performance in four European countries. Complete it using the words given in the lists.

PART 1

around   at   downs   so   upward   of

First, let's have a look at this graph, which shows us the ups and 1) . . . . in the 'footsie' over the last three months. As you can see, the overall trend is (2) . . . . with the index finishing up (3) . . . . (4) . . . . 3,200 in mid-May. This trend, however, can't hide the fact that there was a fall (5) . . . . some eighty points or (6) . . . . between the middle of February and the beginning of March. We'll be looking at the reasons for this unexpected dip in a moment.

LONDON

PART 2

at   about   of   over   to   from

In Paris it's been the same story, with the CAC falling (1) . . . . just (2) . . . . 1850 in mid-February (3) . . . . (4) . . . . 1720 three weeks later. Again, though, overall performance has been good, the CAC putting on roughly 120 points over the three-month period, peaking (5) . . . . just short (6) . . . . 2020, give or take a point.

PARIS

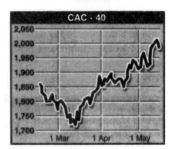

PART 3

down   between   over   of   by   downward

MILAN

As you can see, the picture in Milan is rather different. The early trend was decidedly (1) . . . . In fact, the MIBTel had already fallen (2) . . . . in excess (3) . . . . 1400 points by mid-March.

It then fluctuated (4) . . . . 9700 and 9300 for the best part of a month, before partially recovering to end up well (5) . . . . a hundred points (6) . . . . on the figure for mid-February.

PART 4

for   in   below   near   down   up

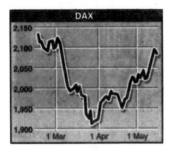

FRANKFURT

If anything, the DAX has fared rather worse. In mid-February it was well (1) . . . . at getting on (2) . . . . 2200 and looking strong. But by the end of March it was way (3) . . . . the 1950 threshold and nowhere (4) . . . . where our forecasts had put it. And it's still well (5) . . . . at somewhere (6) . . . . the region of 2080.

TASK 2

Now try to remember some of the phrases from the presentation which could be of use to you:

1. . . . . and downs
2. a rise of . . . . . . ten points
3. give or . . . . a point
4. just . . . . of 2000
5. the . . . . . . part of a week

6. the overall . . . .
7. an unexpected . . . .
8. in the . . . . of 1080
9. a couple of weeks . . . .
10. getting . . . . . . for 1800

Source of graphs: The European

PRESENTATION

Complete the visuals below with information relevant to your work, company or interests. Make a few notes on each before you present them. You don't need to describe the visuals in detail. Give approximate figures and point out the overall trends and developments.

notes . . . .
. . . .
. . . .
. . . .
. . . .
. . . .
. . . .
. . . .
. . . .
. . . .

notes . . . .
. . . .
. . . .
. . . .
. . . .
. . . .
. . . .
. . . .
. . . .
. . . .

notes . . . .
. . . .
. . . .
. . . .
. . . .
. . . .
. . . .
. . . .
. . . .

USEFUL WORDS AND EXPRESSIONS			
just over	just under	well over	well under
about / around	approximately	roughly	more or less
in the region of	getting on for	just short of	nowhere near

Cause, Effect and Purpose

As a presenter, your job is not just to present *facts*, but also to explain the *reasons* behind the facts and their likely *causes* and *effects*.

English has a lot of expressions which are used to link cause, effect and purpose, but these are mostly used in written reports. The language used in presentations is often much simpler. Compare the following:

REPORT	PRESENTATION
TQM was introduced **in order to** increase efficiency.	We introduced TQM **to** increase efficiency.
The introduction of TQM **led to** a 20% increase in efficiency.	We introduced TQM **and** efficiency increased by 20%.
The 20% increase in efficiency **was a result of** the introduction of TQM.	Efficiency increased by 20% **because** we introduced TQM.

Notice also how noun phrases (the introduction of TQM, a 20% increase in efficiency) are more common in reports, and verb phrases (we introduced TQM, efficiency increased by 20%) are more common in speech.

TASK 1

Look at the following extracts from a report. Change them into what you might say in a presentation, using *and*, *because* and *to*. Remember to change noun phrases into verb phrases where possible. The first words are given:

1. TV coverage of the launch led to a significant increase in customer response rate.

   The launch . . . .

2. There has been a dramatic fall in operating costs as a result of last year's efforts.

   Operating costs . . . .

3. Product modifications may be needed in order to remain internationally competitive.

   We . . . .

4. Market entry was successful due to our competitive pricing strategy.

   We . . . .

5. Investment was increased so as to take advantage of the upturn in the economy.

   We . . . .

6. The slowdown in growth was caused by a loss of corporate confidence.

   Growth . . . .

TASK 2

Sort the following expressions:

| thanks to | brought about | gave rise to | can be traced back to |
| accounts for | owing to | resulted in | is attributable to |

CAUSE (because. . . .)	EFFECT (and . . . .)

PRESENTATION

Present the graph below. Don't worry about quoting precise dates and figures, but pay particular attention to the language of cause, effect and purpose. Remember, *and*, *because* and *to* are usually the only words you will need. The graph has labels to help you.

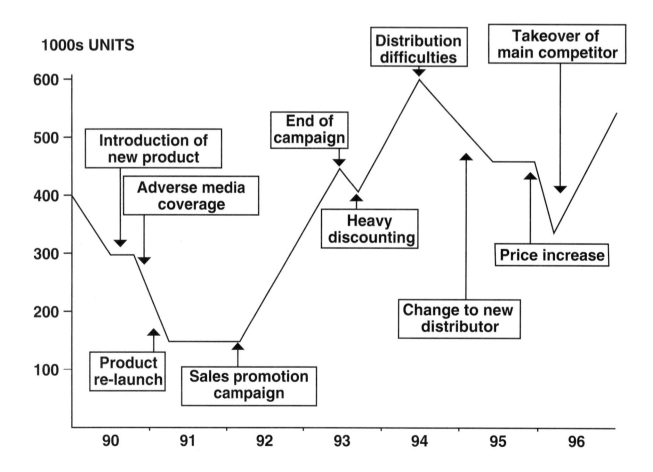

30

Using Your Voice

How to speak in public to create the effect you want, using techniques for highlighting, pausing and stressing

"Perhaps I'd better go over that again . . . . . . in more detail."

Articulation 1

> Make sure you know how to say any long or technical words you may need. In English some parts of a word sound weak, some strong and some very strong.
>
> eg. presen**TA**tion   eco**NO**mical   produc**TI**vity   tech**NO**logy
>
> It is particularly important to know which part of the word has the strongest stress. Bad stress is more likely to make you difficult to understand than bad pronunciation.

`cass` ## TASK 1

Highlight the part of each word which has the strongest stress. The first one has been done for you as an example.

1. presen<u>ta</u>tion
2. collaboration
3. negotiation
4. recommendation
5. decision
6. expansion
7. supervision
8. technician
9. politician
10. optional
11. provisional
12. unconditional

Check the answers in the key. Where does the stress come in words ending in *-ion(al)*, and *-ian*? Can you think of any similar words?

The cassette provides a good model for you. Use it to check your answers after you have done the exercise.

`cass` ## TASK 2

Do the same with these:

1. strategic
2. dynamic
3. systematic
4. problematic
5. bureaucratic
6. typical
7. analytical
8. economical

Check in the key. Where does the stress come in words ending in *-ic(al)*? Can you think of any similar words?

`cass` ## TASK 3

Do the same with these:

1. efficient
2. deficient
3. sufficient
4. proficient
5. experience
6. inconvenience
7. efficiency
8. deficiency

Check in the key. Where does the stress come in words ending in *-ient, -ience* and *-iency*? Can you think of any similar words?

cass **TASK 4**

Do the same with these:

1. essential   2. potential   3. beneficial   4. commercial

5. gradual   6. individual   7. actual   8. eventual

Check in the key. Where does the stress come in words ending in *-ial* and *-ual*? Can you think of any similar words?

cass **TASK 5**

1. flexible   2. incredible   3. impossible   4. probability

5. responsibility   6. productivity   7. modify   8. diversify

Check in the key. Where does the stress come in words ending in *-ible, -ity* and *-ify*? Can you think of any similar words?

cass **TASK 6**

1. obvious   2. ambitious   3. industrious   4. spontaneous

5. simultaneous   6. instantaneous   7. ambiguous   8. superfluous

Check in the key. Where does the stress come in words ending in *-ious, -eous* and *-uous*? Can you think of any similar words?

9. trainee   10. employee   11. guarantee   12. interviewee

Check in the key. Where does the stress come in words ending in *-ee*? Can you think of any similar words?

> Notice that in long words the third to last syllable is frequently stressed:
> technology   simultaneous
> Notice that negative prefixes (un-, in-, im- etc) do not change the way a word is stressed.

TASK 7

Keep a record below of 10 longer words you use a lot in your work or field of interest. Mark the stress in each word and make sure you know exactly how to say it.

Articulation 2

Many of the business words you already know will combine to form useful phrases or *word partnerships*:

market share **sales forecast** **bank charges** **product manager**
do business **cut prices** **recruit staff** **raise productivity**

Learning lots of word partnerships, instead of just words, reduces the amount of thinking you have to do in a presentation. It also helps you to sound more fluent and businesslike. But it is important to know which word in a word partnership is *stressed.*

cass **TASK 1**

Underline the stressed word in each of these partnerships. They are all noun-noun partnerships. The first one has been done for you as an example.

1. <u>cost</u> control
2. sales volume
3. production team

4. price war
5. parent company
6. board meeting

7. profit margin
8. trade barriers
9. marketing mix

10. consumer spending
11. market share
12. market forces

Check the answers in the key. Which word is usually stressed in noun-noun partnerships? Three of the word partnerships above are different. Which ones?

Now do the same with these verb-noun partnerships:

13. fix prices
14. process orders
15. promote sales

16. reduce costs
17. train staff
18. fund research

19. agree terms
20. offset costs
21. market products

22. give discounts
23. quote figures
24. talk money

Check in the key. Which word is usually stressed in verb-noun partnerships?

Do the same with these adjective-noun partnerships:

25. net profit
26. corporate client
27. multinational company

28. fixed assets
29. technological lead
30. economic outlook

31. annual report
32. managerial skills
33. free trade

34. low profitability
35. scientific research
36. cultural awareness

Check in the key. Which word is usually stressed in adjective-noun partnerships?

cass TASK 2

Now do the same with these noun-and-noun partnerships:

1. research and development
2. stocks and shares
3. time and motion
4. training and development
5. aims and objectives
6. trial and error
7. pros and cons
8. ups and downs
9. ins and outs

Check in the key. Which word is usually stressed in noun-and-noun partnerships?

cass TASK 3

Now underline the letter which is stressed in the following:

1. USA
2. UN
3. EU
4. CIA
5. FBI
6. IBM
7. IMF
8. CNN
9. BBC
10. UAE
11. GDP
12. R&D

Check in the key. Which letter is usually stressed in the examples above? Do you know what they mean? Which ones are used in your country?

cass TASK 4

Now try these longer word partnerships. Underline the stressed words.

1. increase profit margins
2. employ temporary staff
3. enter foreign markets
4. create new opportunities
5. annual sales figures
6. competitive performance record
7. stock market report
8. high-technology industry
9. long-term goals
10. far-reaching consequences

Which of the word partnerships above are useful to you?
Write their equivalents in your own language.

English	Translation

35

Chunking 1

> To give an effective presentation in English you must learn to think and speak not in individual words, but in *complete phrases*. This means pausing in the right places:
>
> | INTERESTING | DULL |
> |---|---|
> | **ANYONE** can become a successful **manager.** But, of course, the **unprepared,** the **untrained,** and those given too much **responsibility** before they're **ready** will **FAIL.** **That's** what this morning's **presentation** is all **about.** | Anyone can become a successful manager. But, of course, the unprepared, the untrained, and those given too much responsibility before they're ready will fail. That's what this morning's presentation is all about. |
>
> The ability to present information in *comprehensible chunks* is by far the most important presentation skill you need.

`cass` **TASK 1**

Look at the following presentation extract:

> There's one area of business where the best will always find a job. And it's so vital to the economy that its future is almost guaranteed. The true professional in this field has nothing to fear from technology or the changing marketplace. In fact, they can virtually name their own salary as they provide an essential service, without which most companies would simply go out of business. I'm talking, of course, about selling.

1. Read the extract aloud. If you can, record yourself.
2. Play back your recording. How does it sound? What problems did you have?
3. Now listen to the model extract on your cassette and mark the pauses (/).
4. Listen again and highlight the stressed words.
5. Now try reading the extract and record yourself again. Compare recordings.

Notice how the stressed words tend to be nouns and verbs – the content words.

Notice also how it is generally better to pause after stressed, not unstressed, words.

`cass` **TASK 2**

Do the same with the following extract:

> If the free market is so efficient, why, in terms of its environmental consequences, is the global economy so inefficient? The answer is simple. Marketers are brilliant at setting prices, but quite incapable of taking costs into account. Today we have a free market that does irreparable damage to the environment because it does not reflect the true costs of products and services. The proposals I will be outlining this afternoon all concern, in one way or another, this fundamental flaw in the free market system.

Chunking 2

Pausing in the wrong place in a presentation sounds like hesitation. But pausing *for effect* in the right place is a powerful technique.

Obviously, there are places where you **can't** pause without destroying the meaning of what you are saying. But how **frequently** you pause is a matter of **choice**.

cass **TASK 1**

The following extract is presented in two different ways. Read it aloud. Remember to:

1. pause briefly at the end of each chunk

2. stress the words in bold (usually with an extra strong stress at the end of each chunk)

3. put no stress on unimportant words like *to, at, of, a* and *the*

1.

I'd **like** you to **look** at these **FIGURES,**
which clearly **indicate** the strategic **importance** of **SOUTH KOREA**
in our **attempt** to **gain** a **foothold** in South-East **ASIA.**

2.

I'd **LIKE** you
to **look** at these **FIGURES,**
which clearly **INDICATE**
the strategic **importance** of **SOUTH KOREA**
in our **attempt** to gain a **FOOTHOLD**
in South-East **ASIA.**

Which extract sounds more fluent? Which sounds more emphatic? Which do you prefer?

cass **TASK 2**

Break the following presentation extract first into small chunks, then into larger ones. Read each version aloud. Which version do you think sounds better?

A company is, in many ways, a political organism. But, as far as I'm concerned, there's no place for political agendas in any company I'm running. So to prevent political and territorial battles breaking out, I have two 'golden rules'. First, I make sure that departments interfere as little as possible in each other's business. And, second, I keep everyone fully informed of developments in all departments. There are no secrets. Once you have secrets in an organization, you start getting into company politics.

Try mixing large and small chunks. Try pausing after single words like *but, so* and *first.*

Chunking 3

> Pausing in the wrong place can change the meaning or make you sound
> unclear. Be especially careful when you use **who** and **which**. For example:
>
> **Half of the people who received a personalized sales letter bought the product.**
>
> This means that not everyone got a personalized letter, but half of those who
> did bought the product. Now read the sentence but with different pauses:
>
> **Half of the people who received a personalized sales letter bought the product.**
>
> Now it means that half of the people got a personalized letter, and they all
> bought the product. Totally different.

cass **TASK 1**

Look at the following presentation extracts. Each contains a statement which can have two
completely different meanings, depending on how you say it. The meanings are explained after
each one. Chunk each statement according to what it means. The first one has been done for
you as an example.

1a. We attended the conference on trade tariffs   in Japan.
     The trade tariffs conference was in Japan.

1b. We attended the conference   on trade tariffs in Japan.
     The conference was about Japanese trade tariffs.

2a. Those who sold their shares immediately made a profit.
     But those who didn't sell immediately, didn't make a profit.

2b. Those who sold their shares immediately made a profit.
     All those who sold their shares made an immediate profit.

3a. The Germans who backed the proposal are pleased with the results.
     The Germans backed the proposal and are pleased with the results.

3b. The Germans who backed the proposal are pleased with the results.
     But the Germans who didn't back it, aren't.

4a. It's time to withdraw the economy models which aren't selling.
     All the economy models should be withdrawn because they aren't selling.

4b. It's time to withdraw the economy models which aren't selling.
     So that we can concentrate on the economy models which **are** selling.

cass **TASK 2**

Now say these for fun, and get used to chunking and stressing in different ways for
different effects.

Half the world doesn't know	how the other half lives.
Half the world doesn't know how	the other half lives.
Ignore	everything I'm telling you.
Ignore everything	I'm telling you.
What is this thing	called love?
What is this thing called	love?
What	is this thing called love?

Stress

As a rule, when you give a presentation in English the stress tends to come at the end of each chunk. But by deliberately placing the main stress at the beginning or in the middle of a chunk you can subtly change the meaning of what you say. Look at the following examples:

The BRITISH will never agree to that.
The British will NEVER agree to that.
The British will never AGREE to that.
The British will never agree to THAT.

Try reading out each example with different stress.

cass **TASK**

In each extract below underline the main stress in the first sentence. The first one has been done for you as an example.

1a. The <u>British</u> will never agree to that. But the Germans just might.

1b. The British will <u>never</u> agree to that. Not in a million years.

2a. Sales are up on last year. But profits have hardly moved at all.

2b. Sales are up on last year. But then that was a particularly bad year.

3a. We may not get the whole contract. But we'll get a good part of it.

3b. We may not get the whole contract. But someone will.

4a. The market may be growing. But our market share certainly isn't.

4b. The market may be growing. But, then again, it might just be a seasonal fluctuation.

5a. I think we're making progress. But some of you may not agree with me.

5b. I think we're making progress. But it's very difficult to say at this stage.

6a. We haven't seen a massive improvement yet. But 2% is quite encouraging.

6b. We haven't seen a massive improvement yet. But we soon will.

7a. Our products sell in Sweden. But they don't sell in Denmark.

7b. Our products sell in Sweden. But they don't sell enough.

8a. It's hard to break into Korea. But not impossible.

8b. It's hard to break into Korea. But harder still to break into Japan.

9a. There are three points I'd like to make. And all three concern senior management.

9b. There are three points I'd like to make. And then I'll hand you over to David.

Pacing

> One simple way of keeping an audience's interest is to vary your speed of speaking. Compare the following:
>
> Bad management costs jobs.
> Bad   management   costs   jobs.
>
> This is probably the single most important thing I've said.
> This   is probably   the single   most important   thing   I've said.
>
> In general, you should slow down to make your most important points. This gives your message time to *sink in.*

cass TASK 1

Listen to your cassette. Which of the following chunked statements don't work? They are all famous business quotes. In the first one it is c which is wrong.

1. a. The person who never made a mistake   never made anything.
    b. The person   who never made a mistake   never   made   anything.
    c. The person who   never made a   mistake   never   made anything.

2. a. Management   problems   always   turn   out   to   be people problems.
    b. Management problems   always turn out   to be people problems.
    c. Management   problems   always turn out   to be people   problems.

3. a. Big companies   are small companies   that succeeded.
    b. Big companies   are   small companies that   succeeded.
    c. Big companies   are small companies that succeeded.

4. a. Hard work never killed anybody,   but worrying about it did.
    b. Hard   work   never   killed   anybody,   but worrying about it did.
    c. Hard work never   killed anybody,   but worrying   about it did.

5. a. Ideas are   like children. Your own are   wonderful.
    b. Ideas are like children.   Your own are wonderful.
    c. Ideas   are like children.   Your own   are wonderful.

6. a. The best advertisement   is a good product.
    b. The best   advertisement   is   a good   product.
    c. The   best   advertisement   is a   good product.

cass TASK 2

Now present the following. Experiment with changing the pace.

1. This has never ever happened before.
2. We keep getting the same result – time after time after time.
3. Believe me, we will win the business – it's only a matter of time.
4. If we'd known then what we know now, we'd never have gone ahead.
5. We were number one then. We're number one now. And we always will be.

Intonation 1

> Once you have mastered the basic technique of pausing and stressing in the right places, you can start to give real expressive power to your presentation by making full use of the rise and fall of your voice.

cass ## TASK 1

Listen to the following presentation extract. Notice how the speaker keeps their voice up or level in the middle of statements, and lets it drop at the end:

As a **business** EVOLVES
it goes through FOUR BASIC STAGES.
And at every **stage** of the **business** LIFE cycle
your **company's** financial **needs** are going to CHANGE.

So, what **are** those FOUR STAGES?

Well, **obviously,** when your **business** is NEW
what you **need** most of ALL
is INVESTMENT **capital**
and a **detailed** BUSINESS **plan.**

But **once** your business is **established** and GROWING
and you've got a **solid** CUSTOMER **base,**
then it's time to look into INVESTMENT
and the proper **use** of your RESOURCES.

Companies that fail to GROW
simply DECLINE.
So as your **business** EXPANDS,
you're almost **certainly** going to **need additional** FINANCING.

And FINALLY,
by the **time** the **business** is MATURE,
you'll **want** to get an **accurate** VALUATION
so that, **should** you WANT to,
you can **sell off** the **company** at a **decent** PROFIT.

TASK 2

Present the above extract until you are happy with the way you sound. Compare your version with the one on the cassette.

> Notice how a dramatic rise in your voice creates anticipation and suspense, but a sharp fall gives weight and finality to what you have just said. Keeping your voice up tells the audience you are in the middle of saying something and mustn't be interrupted. Letting your voice drop lets them know you've completed what you wanted to say.

Intonation 2

> A good presentation involves more than just *giving* information. It also involves *interpreting* that information, showing your listeners exactly what it means, giving it *significance*.
> Your intonation – the rise and fall of your voice – tells your audience exactly what you are thinking. Good intonation lets them see your attitude and your enthusiasm for your subject.
> Monotonous speakers bore an audience. So, a golden rule when you give a presentation is to vary the tone of your voice.

`cass` **TASK 1**

Below are some well-known sayings. Present them, paying particular attention to pausing, stress and the rise and fall of your voice. Remember that in a presentation it is better to vary your voice too much rather than too little.

1. Luck is what happens when preparation meets opportunity.

2. The easier it is to do, the harder it is to change.

3. Teamwork is twice the results for half the effort.

4. Don't let what you can't do interfere with what you can.

5. Humor is always the shortest distance between two people.

6. Anyone can make a mistake, but to really mess things up requires a computer.

7. People always have two reasons for doing things: a good reason and the real reason.

8. People who think they know it all are a pain in the neck to those of us who really do.

9. An expert is someone who knows more and more about less and less until he knows everything about nothing.

10. The human brain starts working the moment you are born and doesn't stop until you stand up to speak in public.

Do you have similar sayings in your own language? (NB No 5 is an American quotation.)

`cass` **TASK 2**

Intonation is a good indicator of how you feel about what you are saying. Look at the following contrasts. Notice how your voice tends to rise when you make a positive point and fall when you make a negative one.

1. We're doing well in Europe, but not in the Middle East.

2. Turnover is down, but productivity is up. And for the second year running.

3. In Mexico we're number one, in Argentina we're number one, in Chile we're number one, but in Brazil we're nowhere.

Sound Scripting 1

The ability to chunk your speech in a presentation may seem complicated at first, but it will quickly become quite natural. With practice, you will be amazed at how much clearer and more fluent you sound. A good way of getting into the habit of chunking is to write out parts of your presentation as you would present them and then read them aloud.

TASK

Copy the following presentation extract onto a PC. Note that this extract is recorded. Use the recording only when you reach unit 3.12.

The world's most popular drink is water. You probably knew that already. After all, it's a basic requirement of life on earth. But did you know that the world's second most popular drink is Coke? And that the human race drinks six hundred million Cokes a day? Now, let's just put that into some kind of perspective. It means that every week of every year people drink enough Coke to fill the World Trade Center. In fact, if all the Coca-Cola ever consumed was poured over Niagara Falls instead of water it would take nearly two days to run dry. There's almost nowhere on the planet, from Miami to Malawi, where the word Coke isn't instantly recognized. The brand name alone is worth thirty billion dollars. And that's what makes Coca-Cola a global marketing phenomenon.

Now go back and decide where you would pause for best effect. Press RETURN for each pause. Remember, longer chunks sound more fluent; shorter chunks, more emphatic. Then compare your version with the one below:

The world's most popular drink

is water.

You probably knew that already.

After all,

it's a basic requirement of life on earth.

But did you know

that the world's second most popular drink

is Coke?

And that the human race drinks

six hundred million Cokes a day?

Now, let's just put that into some kind of perspective.

It means

that every week

of every year

people drink enough Coke

to fill the World Trade Center.

In fact,

if all the Coca-Cola ever consumed

was poured over Niagara Falls

instead of water

it would take nearly two days to run dry.

There's almost nowhere on the planet,

from Miami

to Malawi,

where the word Coke

isn't instantly recognized.

The brand name alone

is worth thirty billion dollars.

And that's what makes Coca-Cola

a global marketing phenomenon.

Sound Scripting 2

After knowing where to pause, knowing which words to stress is the most important skill you need when you are presenting to an audience.

TASK

Complete the sound script from the previous unit on your PC by:

1. changing all the stressed words into bold
2. printing in CAPITALS the heavily stressed words (especially at the end of each chunk and for contrast)

Then compare your version with the one below:

The **world's** most **popular** DRINK
is WATER.
You **probably knew** that ALREADY.
After **all,**
it's a basic **requirement** of **life** on EARTH.
But **did** you KNOW
that the world's SECOND most **popular drink**
is COKE?
And that the **human race** drinks
six hundred million Cokes a DAY?
Now, **let's** just **put** that into some **kind** of PERSPECTIVE.
It MEANS
that EVERY WEEK
of EVERY YEAR
people **drink** enough COKE
to **fill** the World TRADE Center.
In FACT,
if **all** the Coca-Cola ever CONSUMED
was **poured** over **Niagara Falls**
instead of WATER
it would **take** nearly TWO DAYS to run DRY.
There's almost nowhere on the PLANET
from MIAMI
to MALAWI,
where the word COKE
isn't **instantly** RECOGNIZED.
The **brand name** ALONE
is worth THIRTY BILLION DOLLARS.
And that's what makes COKE
a GLOBAL MARKETING PHENOMENON.

Sound Scripting 3

Once you are pausing and stressing effectively, start working on your voice and pacing.

cass TASK 1

Complete the sound script from the previous unit on your PC by:

    spacing out   the words   you want   to deliver   slowly

Then compare your version with the one below:

The **world's** most **popular** DRINK

is WATER.

You **probably knew** that ALREADY.

After **all,**

it's a basic **requirement** of **life** on EARTH.

But **did** you KNOW

that the world's SECOND   most **popular drink**

is COKE?

And that the **human race** drinks

six   hundred   million   Cokes a DAY?

Now, **let's** just **put** that into some **kind** of PERSPECTIVE.

It MEANS

that EVERY   WEEK

of EVERY   YEAR

people **drink** enough COKE

to **fill** the World TRADE Center.

In FACT,

if **all** the **Coca-Cola** ever CONSUMED

was **poured** over **Niagara** FALLS

instead of WATER

it would **take**   nearly   TWO   DAYS   to run DRY.

There's almost nowhere on the PLANET

from MIAMI

to MALAWI,

where the word COKE

isn't **instantly** RECOGNIZED.

The **brand name** ALONE

is worth   THIRTY   BILLION   DOLLARS.

And that's what makes COKE

a GLOBAL   MARKETING   PHENOMENON.

TASK 2

Now sound script an extract from a presentation of your own. If you have an overhead projector, copy the text onto a transparency, project it and present it from the screen. This is easier to deliver well because you need to look up, not down at a piece of paper. Ask a colleague to listen to you and tell you what they think. Continue until you feel comfortable with the pacing, rhythm and stress of natural spoken English.

Basic Techniques

Simple techniques to help you communicate your message to maximum effect

"It's nice to see so many of you, but I've only got 20 samples."

Emphasis 1

You can dramatically change the significance of what you say in a presentation by stressing words which would normally be unstressed or contracted. Look at the following examples:

Neutral Remark	**Emphatic Remark**
It's our best chance of success.	It **is** our best chance of success.
We were hoping for a better deal.	We **were** hoping for a better deal.
We're doing the best we can.	We **are** doing the best we can.
We've tried to limit the damage.	We **have** tried to limit the damage.
We can't go ahead with this.	We **cannot** go ahead with this.
I see what you mean.	I **do** see what you mean.
They promised completion by June.	They **did** promise completion by June.
It isn't cost-effective.	It's **not** cost-effective.
Do we or don't we believe in service?	Do we or do we **not** believe in service?

Notice how the auxiliary verbs *(is, are, was, were, has, have, had)* and negatives carry a lot of the emphasis.

cass TASK

Now change the following presentation extracts to emphasize the main points. The first one has been done for you as an example.

1. It's been an exceptional year.   > It **has** been an exceptional year.
2. It's difficult to see what the underlying trend is.
3. We'll get the price we want in the end.
4. $10,000 isn't worth worrying about.
5. We don't see any need for further injections of cash.
6. They promised to have the feasibility study completed by now.
7. Have we or haven't we enjoyed ten years of sustained growth?
8. I'd just like to say that we'll be reviewing the whole situation in six months' time.
9. Look, we've been through all this before and we aren't going through it all again.
10. We offered them an apology and we'd hoped that would be the end of the matter.
11. We were hoping to reach an agreement by May, but that isn't going to be possible now.
12. We appreciate the need to take risks, but we have our shareholders to think of too.
13. We understand the pressure you're all working under, but we've got a business to run, you know.
14. We weren't aware of any change in the bank's circumstances, but I think we should have been informed.
15. The loss of 4% of our business to the Austrians isn't a serious matter, but it's serious enough to demand our attention this morning – so, what's going on?

Read the extracts aloud until you are happy with the way you sound. The cassette provides a good model for you. Use it to check your answers after you have done the exercise.

Emphasis 2

> You can make a presentation more persuasive by using simple *intensifiers* to emphasize your points. Look at the following examples:
>
> I'm afraid it <u>just</u> isn't good enough – the <u>entire</u> system needs updating.
> We <u>really</u> need to rethink our <u>whole</u> recruitment procedure.
> Paying off <u>such</u> a substantial loan is going to be <u>extremely</u> difficult.
> We've done <u>much</u> better than we expected – <u>even</u> better than we did last year.
> There's <u>absolutely</u> no chance <u>at all</u> of us going into profit in the first two years.
> We now lead the market, even though it's still <u>so highly</u> competitive.

`cass` **TASK**

Read the following presentation extracts. First, decide where you could add extra emphasis. Then write in the intensifiers given at the end of the sentence. The first one has been done for you as an example.

extremely	even

1. We're doing ▲ well now. But how can we do ▲ better?   **(extremely, even)**

2. The project is underfunded.   **(whole, badly)**

3. It's obvious that we made a mistake.   **(pretty, terrible)**

4. It works out cheaper to take on casual workers.   **(actually, much)**

5. I'm aware that it's been a disaster from start to finish.   **(fully, total)**

6. I'm certain that we're in a better position now.   **(one hundred percent, significantly)**

7. There's no hope of reaching our targets by the end of phase two.   **(absolutely, at all)**

8. There's been a decrease in demand, and yet sales are up on last year.   **(dramatic, well)**

9. We shouldn't be neglecting a lucrative market.   **(really, such, highly)**

10. There's no chance of making progress.   **(absolutely, whatsoever, real)**

11. It's going to be too expensive to re-equip the factory.   **(just, far, entire)**

12. It's difficult to know whether the figures are going to improve.   **(just, so, actually)**

13. We can't be expected to manage on a tiny budget. It's ridiculous.   **(really, such, just)**

14. It's too late to do anything about it.   **(actually, far, at all)**

Emphasis 3

> Some emphatic expressions are very common in more formal presentations.
> A typical pattern is:
>
> | Subject | Intensifier | Main Verb | Complement |
> |---------|-------------|-----------|------------|
> | I | completely | agree | with everything you've said so far. |
> | We | firmly | oppose | any suggestion that the company be sold. |
>
> Notice that the intensifier and verb form a strong word partnership. It's a
> good idea to learn some of these word partnerships by heart.

TASK

**Match up the three parts of the sentences below to make twelve emphatic expressions.
The first one has been done for you as an example.**

1. We strongly   a. reject   1. any suggestion that we should sell.

2. We totally   b. admit   2. you withdraw the product.

3. We deeply   c. recommend   3. having to lay off 2,000 workers.

4. We freely   d. regret   4. that the buyout was a bad idea.

5. We sincerely   e. refuse   1. what the board is trying to do.

6. We enthusiastically f. accept   2. that profits will continue to recover.

7. We utterly   g. endorse   3. that there will have to be changes.

8. We readily   h. hope   4. to back down on this crucial issue.

9. We categorically   i. encourage   1. that this is in everyone's interests.

10. We fully   j. believe   2. having anything to do with it.

11. We positively   k. deny   3. the difficulties they've been having.

12. We honestly   l. appreciate   4. initiative-taking at all levels.

Emphasis 4

Very often in a presentation it's not *what* you say but *how* you say it. You can create dramatically different effects by placing emphasis on particular words and phrases. Look at the following:

This was successful.
This was very **sucCESSful.**
This was **VEry** successful.

Notice how the effect is changed by a change of emphasis.

`cass` **TASK 1**

Say the following in two different ways:
1. Stress the adjective.   2. Then stress the qualifier (*particularly, hardly* etc).
What's the difference in effect in each case?

1. The results were particularly disappointing.
2. The risks are extremely high.
3. The figures are hardly encouraging.
4. The project is almost complete.
5. We all know that this is a really difficult market.
6. I'm afraid their initial offer was totally unacceptable.
7. The whole thing is virtually impossible.
8. Explaining the situation to head office is going to be rather difficult.
9. Implementing the plan might be slightly problematic.
10. I'm afraid we can't be absolutely certain.

`cass` **TASK 2**

Another way of emphasizing a point is to stress the definite article preceding it:
Not It's the business to be in.   but It's **theee** business to be in.
Notice how *the* sounds *longer* and *stronger*.
In the following presentation extracts decide which *the* should be stressed and highlight it:

1. It's the business opportunity of the year.
2. The Jaguar isn't just an executive car – it's the executive car.
3. It's the single biggest market as far as the telecommunications industry is concerned.
4. When it comes to fast-moving consumer goods, the Koreans are the people to talk to.
5. A joint venture may not turn out to be the solution, but it's the best solution for now.
6. The fact is, we're not just experts – we're the experts in the field.
7. Floating the company on the stock exchange is probably the best thing we ever did.

Two of the statements above are nonsense unless you stress *the*; which ones?
Say the sentences several times, paying particular attention to the way you stress them.

Emphasis 5

> When you present an argument, it often helps to give more than one reason for it and to make it clear what the most important reasons are.

TASK 1

Divide the following expressions into those which introduce an additional point and those which emphasize a point.

1. **Plus**. . .
2. Above **all**, . . .
3. In **particular**, . . .
4. What's **more**, . . .
5. In **addition**, . . .

6. What's **especially** important is . . .
7. But there's **more** to it than **that** . . . .
8. It's **also** a **matter** of . . .
9. I'd like to **emphasize** . . .
10. The **main** thing is . . .

ADDING	EMPHASIZING

TASK 2

Match up the following to make four additional remarks:

It's not JUST that KAJIMA are ONE of the BIGGEST CONSTRUCTION COMPANIES in JAPAN. We ALSO need to . . . .

1. remember   a. account of the fact that construction is Japan's fifth industry.

2. remind   b. in mind that they are consistently in Japan's corporate top fifty.

3. bear   c. that they are one of our best customers.

4. take   d. ourselves of what this firm was like before we got their business.

52

TASK 3

Look at the following emphasis pattern. Complete the adjectives by writing in the missing vowels.

| I can't emphasize **enough** just how | 1. d _ ff _ c _ lt
2. c r _ t _ c _ l
3. r _ s k y
4. _ m p r _ c t _ c _ l
5. _ m p _ r t _ n t
6. v _ t _ l | 7. d _ n g _ r _ _ s
8. _ s s _ n t _ _ l
9. s _ g n _ f _ c _ n t
10. _ n c _ n v _ n _ _ n t
11. p r _ b l _ m _ t _ c
12. c r _ c _ _ l | this | is.
was.
has **been**.
will **be**.
would **be**.
might **be**. |

Which of the adjectives above mean the same as *important*?
Say each expression several times. Concentrate on pausing and stress.

PRESENTATION

Here is a list of qualities needed by a good manager. Present this information, adding and emphasizing points. Emphasize the points which are marked like this *.

The ideal manager should:

be able to take responsibility and make decisions
be able to delegate
be a good communicator*
be confident and assertive
be able to motivate people*
be up to date with the latest developments in their field
keep calm when everyone else panics*

Now do the same for your own job. Emphasize the two or three most important points you make.

In my line of work you need to:

1. ....

2. ....

3. ....

4. ....

5. ....

6. ....

7. ....

8. ....

Focusing

> If you really want to get the attention of your audience, simple emphasis may not be enough. In English there is a way you can focus key points so that everyone knows you want them to listen to what you have to say next. Look at these examples:
>
> We can't expect too much too soon.
> **What we can't do** is expect too much too soon.
>
> I'd like to approach this question from two different angles.
> **What I'd like to do** is approach this question from two different angles.
>
> Notice how the **'What ... is ...'** pattern builds up the anticipation of the audience.

cass TASK 1

Focus the following in the same way to draw the attention of the audience:

1. I'm going to talk about motivation.

   . . . .

2. I'd like to move on to the question of cashflow.

   . . . .

3. I've tried to put our recent difficulties into some kind of perspective.

   . . . .

4. We have to consider what the start-up costs might be.

   . . . .

5. I'll be making a case for getting in a team of specialists.

   . . . .

6. I'd like you to ask yourselves a simple question.

   . . . .

7. We're aiming to be back in the black by the end of this accounting period.

   . . . .

8. I'm going to be looking at the arguments against networking.

   . . . .

9. We found out how pirate copies of the CD were getting into stores.

   . . . .

10. I want to know how long it'll be before we start seeing a profit.

    . . . .

cass **TASK 2**

Now try these. Add the words you need to focus the second statement. Highlight the words you would stress.

1. We want higher productivity. What we . . . . is higher costs.

2. We've increased sales. What . . . . is increase turnover.

3. We're in a good position to improve working conditions. . . . . in a position to do is raise salaries.

4. I'm prepared to discuss the takeover bid. . . . . to do is get into an argument about it.

5. We're not trying to change everything. . . . . to change is this.

6. It doesn't matter how difficult it is. . . . . expensive it is.

PRESENTATION

Complete the following focused statements with information relevant to your work or company. First, choose a topic. Then present each point, paying particular attention to stress and intonation.

TOPIC . . . .
1. What . . . . is . . . .
2. What . . . . is . . . .
3. What . . . . is . . . .
4. What . . . . is . . . .
5. What . . . . is . . . .

1. What I want to know is . . . .
2. What I'm saying is . . . .
3. What I'm trying to say is . . . .

1. We want. . . . .
   What we don't want is . . . .
2. We're trying to . . . .
   What we're not trying to do is . . . .
3. We're in a good position to . . . .
   What we're not in a position to do is . . . .
4. We've been able to. . . . .
   What we haven't been able to do is . . . .
5. It doesn't matter. . . . .
   What does matter is . . . .

Softening 1

> As well as being able to emphasize important points, you sometimes need to reduce the force of points which are of less immediate significance:
>
> | a **great** improvement | > | a **slight** improvement |
> | a **major** problem | > | a **minor** problem |
> | a **total** success | > | a **partial** success |
>
> Look at the following extract from a presentation. See how the highlighted words and phrases have a *softening* effect.
>
> We've <u>more or less</u> completed the first round of negotiations in Osaka, and we're <u>pretty</u> certain they like what we're offering, although with the Japanese it is <u>quite</u> difficult to tell <u>sometimes</u>. It's <u>a little</u> too soon to say whether we'll get an exclusive contract. Exclusivity is <u>probably rather</u> too much to hope for. But we've <u>just about</u> reached agreement on price and, <u>all in all</u>, we're <u>fairly</u> happy with the way things are going.
>
> 'Softeners', like these, are extremely useful when you are uncertain of your facts or want to be diplomatic.

`cass` **TASK**

Read the following presentation extracts. First, decide which words and expressions you could soften. Then write in the 'softeners' given at the end of the extract. The first one has been done for you as an example.

       quite   a little

1. It's not what we wanted, but it's better than their last offer.   **(quite, a little)**
      ▲   ▲

2. I think we're too price-conscious.   **(sometimes, just a little)**

3. I'd say we'll manage to break even.   **(all in all, just about)**

4. It's a good idea, but it's certain to meet opposition.   **(basically, almost)**

5. I'm pleased with our performance and it's been a good year.   **(fairly, all in all, quite)**

6. In Northern Europe the response to our mailshots has been poor and I think that's the result of deciding to target only large firms.   **(generally, rather, partly)**

7. We've done better than we expected this year, although I have to say that net profits are still low.   **(probably, a bit, rather)**

8. We had a few hiccups during the launch and it's been hard work getting the advertising right, but everything's OK now.   **(minor, pretty, more or less)**

9. The procedure is foolproof. If we do make errors of judgement, they're easy to put right.

    (virtually, occasionally, slight, usually, fairly)

Softening 2

When people in the audience make negative remarks about the information you're presenting, you can often soften the impact by restating their point in a more positive way.

cass TASK

Complete the diplomatic responses below by choosing words from the lists:

happy	easy	growing	encouraging	sorry
success	admit	need	grant	true

1. These figures are very disappointing.
   > Well, they're certainly not very . . . . , I have to . . . .

2. The shareholders are going to be furious.
   > Well, they certainly aren't going to be very . . . . , that's . . . .

3. Won't it be difficult to change strategy now?
   > Well, it certainly won't be . . . . , but you don't . . . . me to tell you that.

4. This looks like a declining market to me.
   > Well, it's certainly not a . . . . one, I'll . . . . you that.

5. It seems like the Paris Expo was a total disaster.
   > Well, it certainly wasn't a complete . . . . , I'm . . . . to say.

sure	better	afraid	well	things
point	boom	help	make	pretend

6. These tariffs are going to be a major problem.
   > Well, they're certainly not going to be much of a . . . . , that's for . . . .

7. So, we can expect another slump, then?
   > Well, we certainly can't expect a . . . . , not the way . . . . are going.

8. We just seem to be losing money on this.
   > Well, we certainly don't . . . . any money on it, I'm . . . .

9. We've come out of this pretty badly.
   > Well, we certainly haven't come out of it very . . . . , and there's no . . . .
   denying it.

10. How long can things continue to get worse?
    > Well, they certainly won't get . . . . overnight, and I can't . . . . that
    they will.

Notice in the examples above how the presenter rephrases each negative remark in a positive way. Underline all the fixed expressions in each diplomatic response.

Repetition 1

Simple repetition is one of the good presenter's most powerful techniques. Look at the kind of words which are most effective when repeated:

The overall response has been **much, much** better than anyone ever expected.
It really is **very, very** difficult to predict what might happen in 10 years' time.
It's always **far, far** easier to identify a gap in the market than it is to fill it.

Generally, one repetition works best.

`cass` **TASK 1**

Look at each of the following presentation extracts and highlight the word or words which create a good effect if they are repeated.

1. It's obviously very tempting to close down plants which aren't breaking even.
2. The short-term benefits are obvious, but it's much more difficult to say what the long-term benefits might be.
3. It's way too soon to say just how successful this new initiative has been.
4. There are many reasons why it's very important to get the go-ahead from Brussels.
5. Their demands are absolutely ridiculous and we'll never agree to them.
6. One thing you can be totally sure of: there'll always be a market for quality.

`cass` **TASK 2**

Another common repetition technique is doubling words:

bigger and bigger   better and better   stronger and stronger

What kind of words are they? Highlight the word or words in each of the following presentation extracts which could be doubled.

1. I'm happy to report that our presence in Singapore is getting stronger.
2. As the competition gets tougher, we just get better.
3. As the smaller companies go to the wall, fewer players remain in the market.
4. It's getting harder to make money and easier to lose it.
5. These days more firms are turning to freelance consultants.
6. Over the next ten years management positions are going to become less secure.
7. As new technology moves faster, data protection becomes more of a problem.
8. More people are fighting over fewer jobs for less money.

Present each extract several times. Experiment with doubling one, two and three words. Which do you like best? Get into the habit of repeating your most important points.

Repetition 2

> One of the most powerful techniques in a presentation is simple repetition of key points. Sometimes it's not how you say it, but how often you say it that makes the difference.
>
> A common technique is:
>
> Statement > Repetition > Explanation
>
> **We didn't go AHEAD . . . . We didn't go ahead – because we weren't READY.**
>
> Notice which words are stressed. Pausing before the statement is repeated gives it extra impact.

cass TASK 1

Apply the same technique to the following points. Say them first. Then write them down. The first one has been done for you as an example.

1. Sales – up – we spent more – advertising.
   Sales are up . . . . Sales are up because we spent more on advertising.
2. Profits – down – costs – risen.
   . . . .
3. The market – flat – still in recession.
   . . . .
4. Figures – disappointing – we were expecting too much.
   . . . .
5. We need new product – falling behind – competition.
   . . . .
6. We know it won't work – done it before.
   . . . .
7. Price is everything – market – saturated.
   . . . .
8. The prospects – good – established – firm foothold – Europe.
   . . . .

cass TASK 2

Now try these:

1. The time to act – now – while – opportunities – still there.
   . . . .
2. Results – been very encouraging – in spite – difficult circumstances.
   . . . .
3. It's time – change – strategy – before – too late.
   . . . .
4. Easy – take risks – when – not risking – own money!
   . . . .

Repeat this exercise until you feel comfortable with it.

Repetition 3

Look at how a pause and the strong repetition of a single key word can transform a simple remark:

Nobody knows that better than we do – NOBODY.
Everybody makes mistakes – EVERYBODY.

cass **TASK**

Now complete the strong statements below, using the following words. In seven of them the same word will fill both spaces.

no-one	nowhere	everyone	never	nothing
ever	always	no + none at all	no + not one	every + every one

1. . . . . has ever beaten us on price – . . . .
2. . . . . would persuade us to collaborate with the Belgians – . . . .
3. . . . . could be more suitable than the present site – . . . .
4. . . . . American company has succeeded in this market – . . . .
5. . . . . figure was checked and double-checked – . . . .
6. We have . . . . had such a tremendous year – . . . .
7. We must . . . . remember who our real customers are – . . . .
8. Nobody . . . . gets away with overpricing – . . . .
9. We're taking . . . . risks – . . . .
10. We've beaten absolutely . . . . in the market – . . . .

Present the sentences above. Remember to stress the words you wrote in and to pause before the final stressed word.

PRESENTATION

Complete some or all of the following using information relevant to your work, company or interests. Then present each point until you are happy with the way you sound.

1. Nothing . . . . NOTHING.
2. Nobody . . . . NOBODY.
3. Nowhere . . . . NOWHERE.
4. No . . . . NOT ONE.
5. Everything . . . . EVERYTHING.
6. Everybody . . . . EVERYBODY.
7. Every . . . . EVERY ONE.
8. . . . . never . . . . NEVER.
9. . . . . always . . . . ALWAYS.
10. . . . . no . . . . NONE AT ALL.

Further Techniques

How to develop your public speaking style to impress and influence your audience

"It looks as if the bulb's gone!"

Rhetorical Questions 1

It is often more interesting to present your ideas as questions rather than direct statements. Questions involve the audience. They also make your presentation sound more conversational and create anticipation in the minds of your audience.

cass **TASK**

The rhetorical questions below can be used in many different situations. Complete each of them using the following pairs of words:

where + did	how long + making	how + do	how much + is
how + working	what sort + looking	how soon + seeing	what + waiting
what + attribute	where + go	how come + feeling	what + take

1. For the fifth year running we've managed to increase sales volume.
   So, ... did we . . . . it?

2. The opportunities in Eastern Europe are better now than they've ever been.
   So, ... are we . . . . for?

3. We've lost ground to the Swedes both in Scandinavia and at home.
   So, ... do we . . . . from here?

4. We've spent the best part of a year ploughing money back into R&D.
   So, ... can we expect to start . . . . results?

5. This is the third time we've launched a new product, only to have to withdraw it within the first six months.
   So, ... do we have to go on . . . . the same mistakes?

6. The $8 million they offered us is good, but not good enough.
   So, ... of figure are we . . . . for?

7. We offered them a very attractive package, but they turned us down flat.
   So, ... we go wrong?

8. As you know, we launched a strict cost-cutting campaign last year.
   So, ... we're not . . . . the benefits yet?

9. Turnover topped $2 billion again this year.
   So, ... of that . . . . profit?

10. In spite of the recession, the demand for luxury goods is increasing.
    So, ... do we . . . . this to?

11. Unfortunately, this isn't the first time our partners have been in breach of contract.
    So, ... action do we propose to . . . . ?

12. Obviously, we won't see the real results of the reorganization for some time.
    So, ... do we know it's . . . . ?

Present the points several times, paying particular attention to stress and rhythm.

Rhetorical Questions 2

> Sometimes a good way of introducing an emphatic statement is to ask a rhetorical question first:
>
> **So, just how big IS the market?**
> **. . . . eNORmous.**
>
> Notice how the adjective in the question is reinforced with a stronger adjective in the answer. Notice also how the verb and strong adjective are stressed.

`cass` **TASK 1**

Match the rhetorical questions on the left with their one-word answers on the right:

1. So, just how bad IS the situation?	a. . . . . POsitive.
2. So, just how difficult IS it?	b. . . . . unPREcedented.
3. So, just how sure AM I that we can do it?	c. . . . . imPOssible.
4. So, just how competitive ARE we?	d. . . . . specTACular.
5. So, just how good ARE the results?	e. . . . . STATE-of-the-ART.
6. So, just how unusual IS this trend?	f. . . . . unBEAtable.
7. So, just how small IS the risk?	g. . . . . cataSTROphic.
8. So, just how new IS this technology?	h. . . . . NEgligible.

The cassette provides a good model for you. Use it to check your answers after you have done the exercise.

How many of the adjectives above can be preceded by:

    a. absolutely?

    b. practically?

`cass` **TASK 2**

Now look at this pattern:

So, just how bad is the situation?
> I'll tell you how bad it is. It's absolutely catastrophic!

So, just how difficult is it?
> I'll tell you how difficult it is. It's practically impossible.

Notice how the second sentence reinforces the rhetorical question. Reinforce the other rhetorical questions in Task 1 above in the same way.

Now look back at Rhetorical Questions 1 on page 62 and do the same.

Rhetorical Questions 3

> You can make a rhetorical question much more powerful by repeating key words. The following pattern is common:
>
> **Statement + Rhetorical Question + Answer**
>
> **The fact is, cheap imitations of our leading product are flooding the market. So what's the SOLUTION? The SOLUTION is to push for tighter CONTROLS.**
>
> Notice the repetition of *solution* linking question and answer.

cass **TASK**

Complete the presentation extracts below using the following words. In each extract the same word fills both spaces.

answer	point	result
problem	idea	objective
advantages	chances	prospects

1. We've made fifteen different improvements to the basic product and the customers are still complaining.

   So what's the . . . . ? The . . . . is the product itself is out-of-date.

2. We've spent twice as much money marketing the product in Mexico as we have in the States.

   And what's the . . . . ? The . . . . is we've badly neglected the home market.

3. Let's turn to the question of sales targets.

   What's our main . . . . ? Our main . . . . is to reach the three million mark within the next six months.

4. We're still having no luck getting the Brazilians to accept our British cola.

   So what's the . . . . ? The . . . . is to give it an American-sounding name.

5. We keep trying to get a foothold in the European market and we keep failing to do so.

   So what's the . . . . ? The . . . . is we have to sell there if we're to survive.

6. After a lot of hard thinking, we've decided to phase the luxury models out.

   So what's the . . . . ? Well, obviously, the . . . . is to go downmarket.

7. I'd like you now to consider the future of the home computer industry.

   What are the . . . . ? Well, the . . . . are excellent, but only for the right kind of company.

8. We could, of course, increase our marketing budget and try to beat the Japanese at their own game.
But what are our . . . . ? Well, frankly, our . . . . are slim.

9. The obvious disadvantage of setting up in Hungary is its economic situation.
But what are the . . . . ? The . . . . are the low cost of land, an excellent exchange rate, and the possibility of getting government funding for the project.

Present the extracts several times, paying particular attention to stress and rhythm.

PRESENTATION

Complete the following frames using information relevant to your work, company or interests. In each case, first state the situation, then ask and answer a rhetorical question.

1. The situation is this: . . . .

. . . . is / are the . . . . ?

The . . . . is / are . . . .

2. The situation is this: . . . .

. . . . is / are the . . . . ?

The . . . . is / are . . . .

3. The situation is this: . . . .

. . . . is / are the . . . . ?

The . . . . is / are . . . .

4. The situation is this: . . . .

. . . . is / are the . . . . ?

The . . . . is / are . . . .

5. The situation is this: . . . .

. . . . is / are the . . . . ?

The . . . . is / are . . . .

Dramatic Contrasts 1

> Good presenters frequently make use of dramatic contrast to reinforce the point they are making.
>
> **Ten years ago we had a reputation for excellence.**
> **Today we're in danger of losing that reputation.**
>
> **While our competitors have been fighting over the European market, we've been establishing ourselves as market leaders in the Middle East.**
>
> People are very aware of simple opposites – good and bad, past and present, us and them. And if you can make your point with two strongly opposing ideas, you will immediately get the attention of your audience.

cass **TASK**

Match up the two halves of the contrasts below:

1. If we don't take care of the customer,   a. it's a question of money.

2. While our competitors are still doing the feasibility studies,   b. than correcting stupid mistakes later.

3. Instead of just sitting here saying nothing can be done,   c. and an extraordinary one is that little extra.

4. Asking difficult questions now is a lot easier   d. we've actually gone ahead and developed the product.

5. In the 80s the shelf-life of a new PC was three years;   e. or we'll be downsizing by 50% in eighteen months time.

6. Remember, it can take years to win new business,   f. but we went ahead and did it anyway.

7. The only difference between an ordinary manager   g. why don't we get out there and actually do something?

8. Everyone said we'd never do it,   h. but it only takes seconds to lose it.

9. Either we downsize by 25% now   i. these days it might be obsolete in three months.

10. It's not a question of time;   j. someone else will.

Look for patterns in the dramatic contrasts above eg. *If we don't ... , someone else will.*

Notice how many of the extracts above rely on a simple opposition:

       we – someone else   nothing – something   now – later

Notice also how the voice tends to rise on the first half of each contrast and fall on the second.

PRESENTATION

Use the frames below to present information relevant to your own work or company through dramatic contrasts. First, introduce each topic, and then make your point. Repeat this activity until you are happy with the way you sound.

FIRST TOPIC: . . . .
If we don't . . . . , someone else will.

SECOND TOPIC: . . . .
While our competitors . . . .
we . . . .

THIRD TOPIC: . . . .
Instead of just . . . .
why don't we . . . .

FOURTH TOPIC: . . . . now is a lot easier than
. . . . later.

FIFTH TOPIC: . . . .
. . . . ago
Today . . . .

SIXTH TOPIC: . . . .
Remember, it can take . . . . ,
but it only takes . . . .

SEVENTH TOPIC: . . . .
The only difference between a . . . .
and a . . . .

EIGHTH TOPIC: . . . .
Everyone said we'd never . . . . ,
but we . . . .

NINTH TOPIC: . . . .
Either we . . . .
or we . . . .

TENTH TOPIC: . . . .
It's not a question of . . . .
It's a question of . . . .

Dramatic Contrasts 2

> Contrast is one of the the most common presentation techniques. And a lot of famous quotations take the form of dramatic contrasts:
>
> **That's one small step for man. One giant leap for mankind.**
> Neil Armstrong
>
> **The difficult: that which can be done immediately.**
> **The impossible: that which takes a little longer.**
> George Santayana

cass **TASK**

Look at the following famous quotations. Each consists of a dramatic contrast. Can you guess how they finish? The answers are in the key.

1. "Ask not what your country can do for you.
    Ask what you . . . ."   John F. Kennedy

2. "To decide not to decide is a decision.
    To fail to decide . . . ."   Gen. George Patton

3. "It's a recession when your neighbour loses his job.
    It's a depression when . . . ."   Harry S. Truman

4. "If you owe your bank a hundred pounds, you have a problem.
    But if you owe it a million, ..."   J. M. Keynes

5. "Everything has been thought of before.
    The problem is to think . . . ."   Goethe

6. "I like the dreams of the future
    better than the history . . . ."   Thomas Jefferson

7. "I'd rather be a failure at something I enjoy
    than a success at . . . ."   George Burns

8. "Wise men talk because they have something to say;
    fools because they have to . . . ."   Plato

9. "Success is getting what you want.
    Happiness is wanting . . . ."   Benjamin Franklin

10. "Many a man owes his success to his first wife,
    and his second . . . ."   Jim Backus

11. "You can't win them all.
    But you sure can . . . ."   Anonymous

12. "A businessman is someone who talks golf all morning in the office.
    And business all afternoon . . . ."   Anonymous

You probably found a lot of the quotations in this exercise quite easy to complete. Why do you think that was? Say them aloud, paying particular attention to how you say them.

Tripling 1

> Good presenters frequently chunk important points in threes. Look at the following examples:
>
> | | 1 | 2 | 3 |
> |---|---|---|---|
> | **Our service is** | swift, | efficient | and professional. |
> | **What's needed now is** | time, | effort | and money. |
> | **This is how the project is to be** | planned, | organized | and managed. |
>
> Why does this make more impact?

cass ## TASK 1

Say the following. Stress the words in bold type, especially the last word.

1. The new system is **FAST.**
2. The new system is **efficient** and **FAST.**
3. The new system is **foolproof,** **efficient** and FAST.
4. The new system is **economical,** **foolproof,** **efficient** and FAST.

Notice that examples 1 - 3 take about the same time to say. But example 4 is almost impossible to say at normal speed. Three points are usually the most you can comfortably make. Usually you arrange the points so the one you think is most important comes last. Whenever you make important points, remember the 'rule of threes'.

cass ## TASK 2

Match up the statements below:

The ideal		is	
	1. company		a. new, well designed and competitively priced.
	2. project		b. local, expanding and undersupplied.
	3. market		c. thoroughly researched, properly funded and well-run.
	4. product		d. experienced, highly motivated and well-qualified.
	5. manager		e. small, flexible and customer-oriented.

TASK 3

cass Match up these statements:

What you need to		is	
	1. boost sales		a. new plant, proper training and realistic targets.
	2. increase productivity		b. better pay, better conditions and shorter hours.
	3. raise morale		c. determination, imagination and guts.
	4. be an entrepreneur		d. blood, sweat and tears!
	5. build a successful company		e. better service, bigger discounts and lower prices.

Present the points several times, paying particular attention to stress and rhythm.

Tripling 2

> Look at the following presentation extract. Listen to how the voice rises and falls. Notice the simple technique:
>
> | | |
> |---|---|
> | **How did we reach our goals?** | (Rhetorical Question) |
> | **Simple.** | (Short Response) |
> | **By building new plant,** | (Three-Part Answer) |
> | **by taking on more workers,** | |
> | **by keeping production costs down.** | |
>
> Notice also the effect of repetition: '*by building ... by taking ... by keeping*'.

`cass` **TASK 1**

Apply the same technique to the following. Say them first. Then write them down. The first one has been done for you as an example.

1. What / solution? Simple. Cut expenses / staffing levels / salaries.
    What's the solution? Simple. Cut expenses, cut staffing levels, cut salaries.

2. What / answer? Simple. Work harder, / faster, / smarter.
    . . . .

3. Where / best opportunities? It's obvious. In Germany / Japan / Brazil.
    . . . .

4. Can we improve performance? Yes. In terms / output / turnover / profit margin.
    . . . .

5. What would cuts mean / this stage? Disaster! No new plant / new product / new ideas!

    . . . .

6. Change / system and what / you get? Problems. / Problems / workers / distributors / customers.

    . . . .

`cass` **TASK 2**

Now try these:

1. How can we beat the Koreans? I'll tell you. On reliability / quality / price. That's how.
2. Does comparative advertising / results? Of course it does. Ask IBM / Apple / Pepsi / They'll tell you.
3. Can market leadership / achieved / computers? Sure it can. Look / Tom Watson / John Sculley / Bill Gates / They did it.
4. How / we doing? Better than ever. The customers like us / the shareholders / the banks / ! Need I say more?

Present the points above several times, paying particular attention to stress and rhythm. Now try putting the word *and* before the third point in each example. This gives the third point more impact.

PRESENTATION

Use the space below to prepare a mini-presentation of your own, using the tripling pattern. Present three topics relevant to your work, company or interests. First, introduce each topic and then make your point. Repeat this activity until you are happy with the way you sound.

FIRST TOPIC: . . . .

Rhetorical Question: . . . .

Short Response: . . . .

Three-Part Answer: . . . .

(and) . . . .

SECOND TOPIC: . . . .

Rhetorical Question: . . . . ?

Short Response: . . . .

Three-Part Answer: . . . .

(and) . . . .

THIRD TOPIC: . . . .

Rhetorical Question: . . . . ?

Short Response: . . . .

Three-Part Answer: . . . .

(and) . . . .

If possible, copy this completed page onto an overhead transparency and present the points from the screen. Looking up at the screen, instead of down at a piece of paper, will help you to present more clearly.

Tripling 3

> Lists of three are especially memorable. And, throughout history, some of the most famous quotations in all the languages of the world have been lists of three:
>
> Government **of** the people,
> **by** the people,
> **for** the people.   **Abraham Lincoln**
>
> I **came**,
> I **saw**,
> I **conquered**.   **Julius Caesar**
>
> **Tell** me and I **forget**;
> **show** me and I **remember**;
> **involve** me and I **understand**.   **Ancient Chinese proverb**

cass **TASK 1**

Study the following well-known quotations and try to say them so that they have an impact. Mark the pauses with a slash (/) and highlight the words you want to stress. Then listen to your cassette and check.

1. "Never in the field of human conflict was so much owed by so many to so few."

   Winston Churchill

2. "You can fool all the people some of the time and some of the people all the time, but you cannot fool all the people all the time."   **Abraham Lincoln**

3. "What is a committee? A group of the unwilling, picked from the unfit to do the unnecessary."   **Richard Harkness**

4. "People can be divided into three groups: those who make things happen, those who watch things happen and those who ask 'What happened?'"   **John Newbern**

5. "This is not the end. It is not even the beginning of the end. But it is, perhaps, the end of the beginning."   **Winston Churchill**

6. "Coming together is a beginning; keeping together is progress; working together is success."   **Henry Ford**

7. "Organizations don't have new ideas. Teams don't have new ideas. Individuals have new ideas. That's why you come first."   **John Adair**

8. "There are three types of lies: lies, damned lies and statistics."   **Benjamin Disraeli**

9. "The other man's word is an opinion; yours is the truth; and your boss's is law."

   Anonymous

10. "Most presentations have three basic stages: tell them what you're going to tell them; tell them; tell them what you told them." **Anonymous**

11. "The old believe everything; the middle-aged suspect everything; the young know everything." **Oscar Wilde**

12. "All the things I really like to do are either immoral, illegal, or fattening."

Alexander Woollcott

Do you know any famous quotations in your own language which are also lists of three? Make up one of your own.

TASK 2

Now complete the quotations below using the following sets of words:

everyone – fool – computer	today – tomorrow – yesterday
sex – money – power	lead – follow – get
succeed – try – try	nothing – everything – anything

1. COMMITMENT

   If at first you don't . . . . , ... , ... again. Then quit – no use being a damn fool about it!

2. MOTIVATION

   I'm done with . . . . And God knows I've made enough . . . .
   But . . . . , now that's something you never get tired of.

3. INFORMATION TECHNOLOGY

   . . . . makes mistakes. And a . . . . keeps making the same mistakes.
   But to really foul things up you need a . . . .

4. FORWARD PLANNING

   . . . . is the . . . . you worried about . . . .

5. PROJECT MANAGEMENT

   . . . . is as easy as it looks. . . . . takes longer than you think. And if . . . . can go wrong, it will.

6. LEADERSHIP SKILLS

   . . . . , ... or . . . . out of the way.

Machine-Gunning

Three important points seem to be the most an audience can comfortably keep in their heads at one time. And if you make four or five, people will probably forget some of them. But make six or seven or eight points and, although no-one will remember them all, you will impress your audience with the force of your overall argument.

It's **cheaper, newer, faster, bigger, cleaner, safer AND better designed** than **anything else** on the **market. WHAT MORE CAN I SAY?**

Notice how the list of points is delivered at speed with each point stressed to create a machine-gun effect – bang, bang, bang, bang, bang, bang, bang! Notice also the powerful remark at the end.

---

cass TASK 1

Present the extracts below. Remember to machine-gun each point. You will probably need to do this several times. This technique is not for beginners!

1. The new cabriolet is faster, sleeker, smoother, classier, racier, roomier and better-looking than anything else on the market.

2. As a company, we're quite simply more competitive, more creative, more innovative, more responsive, more customer-conscious and more market-driven than any of our competitors.

3. The Middle Eastern market is probably bigger, better, freer, fairer, more liberal and more lucrative than any other market.

4. In terms of performance, we're more motivated, more productive, more profitable, more efficient, more quality-conscious and generally more successful than ever.

5. The home computer industry is likely to be even more technology-driven, more cost-conscious, more price-sensitive, more risk-laden, more overcrowded and more volatile than it is today.

Notice how the presenter repeats certain sounds to heighten the effect:
   faster, sleeker, smoother, classier, racier, roomier . . . .

Notice the frequent repetition of *more*. Notice also how the last point made is usually the most important one.

cass TASK 2

You can increase the force of each statement by adding a powerful remark at the end. Here are some useful ones. Match those with a similar meaning.

1. Need I say more?
2. It's as simple as that.
3. And that's as true now as it's ever been.

a. And that's all there is to it.
b. Always has been, and always will be.
c. What more can I say?

Now try presenting each extract above *slowly* and gradually increase the *volume* of your voice as you speak. This makes what you say more dramatic.

PRESENTATION

Complete whichever of the following frames are relevant to your work, company or interests. Try to include at least six points in support of each statement you make. Don't just write anything. Really think about strong points you would like to make.

---

1. The . . . . is . . . . and . . . . than anything else on the market.

2. As a company, we're quite simply . . . . and . . . . than any of our competitors.

3. The . . . . market is probably . . . . and . . . . than any other market.

4. In terms of . . . . we're . . . . and . . . . than ever.

5. The . . . . industry is likely to be much / far / even . . . . and . . . . than it is today.

Present the above, paying particular attention to speed, rhythm and stress. If you like, finish off each with one of these emphatic expressions:

Need I say more?
What more can I say?

It's as simple as that.
And that's all there is to it.

Always has been, and always will be.
And that's as true now as it's ever been.

Build-ups

> One very effective way of emphasizing a point is to present several connected pieces of information which build up to a short and simple conclusion.
>
> **As far as this contract in the Emirates is concerned, we're pretty tied up with a lot of other projects at the moment, so there's no way we could meet their deadlines. We have very little experience of this kind of work, anyway. And, to be honest, they're not prepared to pay us what we'd want . . . . BASICALLY, it's out of the question.**
>
> The last sentence is a simple summary of the situation in a word or phrase. The main message is clearly delivered after a short pause.

cass **TASK**

Complete the presentation extracts below using the following words and an appropriate summary from the list at the end of the exercise.

access	price	trip	agent
costs	process	business	production
road	requirements	grant	impression
channels	dividends	exchange	stores

1. Sales are up, exports are up, profits are up, shareholders' . . . . are up and . . . . are down.

   . . . .

2. The product presentation went well. We were able to meet all their . . . . , we know they were happy with the . . . . , and frankly I don't think the opposition had made a very good . . . . on them.

   . . . .

3. Rapallo has easy . . . . to the port of Genoa and has good . . . . and rail links with La Spezia, Milan, Turin and the South of France. And as Rapallo is an EU-assisted area, we might be in line for a . . . . to help with start-up costs.

   . . . .

4. I want our reputation to be based on reliability. I want defects eliminated from the production . . . . altogether. I want our products rolling off the . . . . lines, passing through the distribution . . . . and into . . . . at the same rate they are purchased by the customer. That's what I want.

   . . . .

76

5. A number of things have changed since my last report. Two of the companies we visited on our fact-finding . . . . to Mexico have gone out of . . . . We know for a fact that the company we spoke to which showed most interest in our products has taken its business elsewhere. The . . . . rate is very unstable. And we've had no word from our . . . . over there in months.

. . . .

SUMMARIES

a. To put it simply, we're getting nowhere!
b. To put it briefly, it's our best year ever.
c. In a nutshell, the contract is as good as ours.

d. In short, it's the ideal location.
e. In a word, quality.

PRESENTATION

Complete the following frames using information relevant to your work, company or interests. First, present three or four connected facts. Then, sum up the basic message in a word or phrase. Topics you could present include:

The last five years in your industry
Why your company is better than the rest
Your company's current financial position
Your country's current economic situation

The next five years in your industry
The state of the market you operate in
Your place in the market
A best-selling product

---

1. . . . .

. . . .

. . . .

And . . . .

Basically . . . .

2. . . . .

. . . .

. . . .

And . . . .

To put it simply / briefly, ...

3. . . . .

. . . .

. . . .

And . . . .

In short / in a word / in a nutshell, ...

Present each topic. Remember to give the facts fairly quickly and pause before summing up.

Knock-downs

A popular technique with presenters who want to sound provocative is to carefully build up a series of points which seem to oppose their main argument and then knock them all down in a single sentence:

Of course, the experts said that a palm-top computer could never succeed. They did market research which showed that people would just see it as a gimmick. They said its memory capacity would be too limited for serious business users. And they did feasibility studies which showed that the keyboard would be too small for even the fingers of a five-year-old!

So, how come it sold more than a million units in its first year?

Notice how the presenter pauses before delivering the final knock-down.

cass TASK

Complete the presentation extracts below using the following words and an appropriate knock-down from the list at the bottom of the page.

trade	ground	system	model	management	priced
backing	service	competition	access	quality	programs
pursuing	reviews	persuade	storm	confidential	well-established

1. I admit they're a . . . . supplier with a reputation for . . . . and after-sales . . . . Their products are competitively . . . . They're number one in Europe.

2. We prevent unauthorized . . . . to . . . . files in the database by running specially encrypted . . . . Passwords are regularly changed. And we've had a state-of the-art data protection . . . . installed.

3. As you know, it was extremely difficult to . . . . senior . . . . that our idea was worth . . . . And I have to say that we got virtually no financial . . . . for this project because nobody believed we'd ever get it off the . . . .

4. The introduction of the new . . . . took the market by . . . . It received some of the best . . . . we've ever had in the . . . . press. And, in terms of technological innovation, it left the . . . . standing. We were expecting great things.

KNOCK-DOWNS

a. But it didn't stop us going ahead, and to date the project has saved us DM100 million.
b. But what I want to know is, how do they compare with the suppliers we use now?
c. And yet all we did was reduce the market share of our existing product.
d. The problem is that any system is only as secure as the people who use it.

78

PRESENTATION

Complete the following frames using information relevant to your work or company.

    1. First, present three or four points which oppose your main argument.

    2. Pause.

    3. Then, destroy those points in a short knock-down spoken in a louder voice.

Topics you could present include:

> A brilliant idea nobody thought would work
>
> A stupid idea everybody thought would work
>
> A series of mistakes which led to a breakthrough
>
> How doing all the right things led to a disaster
>
> How a new product failed to live up to expectations
>
> How a new product exceeded all expectations

---

1. ....
....
....
....

KNOCK-DOWN: ....

2. ....
....
....
....

KNOCK-DOWN: ....

3. ....
....
....
....

KNOCK-DOWN: ....

Typical Knock-Downs:

So, how come . . . . ?

The problem is . . . . .

The amazing / stupid thing is . . . . .

But it didn't stop us / them . . . . .

But what I want to know is . . . . .

Simplification

As a general rule, the simpler what you say is, the more impact it will have. Sometimes, by cutting out all but the most important words, you can have a powerful effect.

Should we be thinking of expansion? No, that would not be a good idea. Why wouldn't it? Well, that should be obvious. It's much too risky.

Expansion?   Not a good idea.   Why?   Obvious.   Too risky.

Notice the number of unnecessary words. What kind of words are they? Notice the way the voice rises and falls.

cass TASK

Cross out the unnecessary words in the following presentation extracts to create a more powerful effect. Decide yourself exactly how many you cross out. Be careful – if you cross out important words you will change the meaning. The first one has been done for you as an example.

1. ~~Should we be considering a~~ change of strategy? ~~I'm afraid that~~ wouldn't work ~~because there's~~ no time.
   Change of strategy?   Wouldn't work.   No time.

2. If you pack in too many product features, naturally your prices go up and eventually you lose customers.

3. The question is, how are we going to break even? And the answer, I think, is to focus our attention on efficiency.

4. What about diversification? Is it a good idea? Sure, it is. But isn't it a bit too late? Yes, I'm sorry to say, it probably is.

5. In 1981 we were making huge losses. This year we've become the market leader. How do you explain that? It's really very simple. We worked very hard for it.

6. So, we've massively overspent. The answer is to cut back now. But just how are we going to do this? Well, that's easy. There will have to be a wage freeze.

7. So, what about the merger? Do we agree to go ahead with it now? Or do we decide to wait until our position is clearer? Obviously, for the time being we should wait.

8. Basically, we're having three problems. Number one, we don't have the money we need. Number two, we have insufficient experience in this field. And number three, there's far too much competition around.

9. The point is, big companies are out of fashion these days. And it's the small companies who are in. To give you an example, look at IBM. Once they were at the top of the computer industry. Now it's more of a struggle for them.

Present each point until you are satisfied with the way you sound. Concentrate on how your voice rises and falls.

PRESENTATION

Make four simple points about your work, company or interests. Cut out all unnecessary words. Try to include rhetorical questions. These frameworks may help you:

Should we . . . ?	Good idea. Yes. No. Not a good idea.	Why? Why not?	Obvious. Obvious.

Is it . . . ?	Yes. Yes and no. No.	Obviously. Yes, it's . . . Obviously not.	But no, it's not . . .

Can we . . . ?	No problem. Sure. Maybe. I'm afraid not. No way.	(But) how? It depends. Too late / soon / difficult / expensive / . . .	That's easy, . . .

How can we . . . ?	Simple. No idea.	We . . . We can't . . .	And we . . . And we can't . . .

Question . . . Problem . . .	How/why/when . . . ? Not enough/too much . . .		Answer . . . Solution . . .

1. . . . .
. . . .

2. . . . .
. . . .

3. . . . .
. . . .

4. . . . .
. . . .

Present each point several times. Pay special attention to pausing and the rise and fall of your voice.

Creating Rapport 1

Building up a good relationship or rapport with your audience is important, especially in the early stages of your presentation. Personality plays a part, but some simple language patterns help.

1. **Use the words** *we (all), us (all), our* **and** *ours* **as much as possible.**
   Basically, <u>we all</u> share the same goal. And <u>our</u> goal is increased profit.
2. **Use question tags to push for agreement.**
   And we all know what that means, <u>don't we</u>?
3. **Use negative question forms to appeal to your audience.**
   <u>Haven't we all</u> had similar experiences at one time or another?

These involve your audience. Remember eye contact is also important.

TASK 1

Change some of the pronouns to *we (all), us (all), our, ours* and *ourselves* etc.

1. I'm sure the implications of the proposed merger are clear to all of you.
2. I want you to be thinking of ways in which you can maximize sales.
3. I'm aiming to turn the losses you've been making into profits within eighteen months.
4. You know from your own experience how difficult it is to re-establish yourself in an overseas market.
5. I think you need to ask yourselves how long you can go on exceeding your budget.

Sometimes you want to make a distinction between *me* and *you*, but you build rapport by talking about US whenever you can.

`cass` TASK 2

Add question tags to these:

1. We have to reorganize if we're to survive. And that won't be easy.
2. It isn't really a question of marketing. It's more a question of product management.
3. Clearly, the results are better than we expected. But then we weren't expecting much.
4. We've all talked about this before. And I don't think we've ever reached a proper decision. Still, that's not surprising, given the circumstances.
5. We can't really blame our poor performance on the local economy. Because that's supposed to be improving. But what we can do is look at global trends.

Whenever you use question tags to gain rapport, make sure your voice drops at the end. Falling intonation suggests confidence. Rising intonation suggests uncertainty.

`cass` TASK 3

Look at the presentation extracts below and rephrase them as negative questions.

1. It's about time we took a fresh look at packaging.
2. I told you we'd exceed our targets. We always do.
3. We're fortunate to have weathered the recession as well as we have.
4. We want shorter hours. We want better conditions. We want higher pay.
5. There's a need for more teamwork. This is something we should be looking at.

Creating Rapport 2

> Using a few simple words and phrases which do not mean very much in themselves will change the whole tone of your presentation and make it less formal and more friendly.

`cass` **TASK 1**

Look at the following extract from a presentation on the advantages of setting up a business in Dubai. What do you think is the purpose of the words and phrases in bold?

1. **You know,** over the past four years more than five hundred international companies have **actually** set up in Dubai.

2. **You see,** it's a rapidly developing market. True, it's only a small member state of the UAE. But it's also the gateway to a vast geographic area that's worth well over a hundred billion dollars in annual imports.

3. **As a matter of fact,** in the last four years Dubai's imports have more than doubled. And it currently enjoys economic growth of around 6%.

4. **Now**, that's about the same as the USA, Japan and Germany put together!

5. Clearly, **then,** Dubai has enormous potential.

6. But what are the immediate benefits? **Well,** for one thing, it's a totally tax-free zone.

7. **So,** no corporation or income tax to worry about.

8. And for another, it's **actually** an extremely liberal trading nation with no trade barriers, no foreign exchange controls and low or zero import duties. **OK?**

9. **OK, so** what about telecommunications and travel?

10. **Well,** Dubai Telecom is state-of-the-art. The country has a first-class infrastructure. And a hundred shipping lines and sixty-five airlines connect it with the outside world.

TASK 2

Which of the words and phrases in the previous exercise have the following purposes? Highlight them. In some cases there may be more than one answer.

1. Stop. Move on.	a. well	b. OK, so	c. actually
2. Good question.	a. actually	b. so	c. well
3. I want to tell you something.	a. you know	b. then	c. OK?
4. This is important.	a. well	b. you see	c. you know
5. This may seem surprising.	a. actually	b. you see	c. OK?
6. This supports my last point.	a. OK, so	b. then	c. as a matter of fact
7. Therefore.	a. so	b. well	c. then
8. Can we move on?	a. OK, so	b. OK?	c. well
9. Let me think.	a. actually	b. then	c. now

83

Creating Rapport 3

> Many of the best presentations sound more like conversations. So, during your talk, try to keep referring back to your audience as individuals. There are a lot of expressions you can use which help you to do this. Use them regularly and you can make even a more formal presentation sound conversational.

cass **TASK 1**

Match up the following to make a complete presentation extract. Then highlight the most useful expressions.

1. If you're anything like me,

2. And if I were to ask you what makes a successful entrepreneur,

3. Now, I know what you're thinking.

4. But, you see,

5. Because there aren't any secrets.

6. Let me ask you something.

a. that's just where you're wrong.

b. And in many ways, all of us are already entrepreneurs.

c. When was the last time you did something without clearing it with the boss, because it was quicker?

d. you'd probably say it's 90% luck.

e. you'd never dream of calling yourself an entrepreneur.

f. You're thinking: oh no, here we go. He's going to tell us the secrets of entrepreneurship.

cass **TASK 2**

Now do the same with these:

1. Exactly. I can see some of you

2. Because I'm sure everyone in this room

3. It's true, isn't it? Given the chance, most of us are happy to take risks and initiatives. Do you see

4. Now, I'm sure you don't need me to tell you

5. And it's certainly true that good managers don't necessarily make good entrepreneurs.

6. And we all know what that means,

a. don't we? No promotion prospects.

b. there's a lot more to entrepreneurism than the ability to take risks.

c. But isn't it also true that it's often the really enterprising managers who find it hardest to fit in?

d. has gone behind their boss's back at some time or another.

e. what I mean? Everyone has an entrepreneur inside them, fighting to get out.

f. know what I'm talking about.

Key Language

The most important expressions to help you with the content of your presentation

"So, the results were bad."
"Well, they weren't very good."

Business Terms 1

> An important part of preparing your presentation is to decide precisely what topics you are going to discuss and what words you are likely to need to discuss them.

TASK 1

Complete the following statements with information which is relevant to your work or company, by first filling in the gaps and then highlighting the most suitable positive or negative adjective or adding one of your own.

1. The . . . . market in . . . . is
   EXPANDING / BUOYANT / FLAT / SATURATED.

2. Sales of . . . . in . . . . are
   BOOMING / SLUGGISH / STATIC / DECLINING.

3. Business in . . . . is
   THRIVING / BRISK / SLOW / SLACK.

4. The . . . . economy is
   STRONG / SOUND / STABLE / WEAK.

5. The . . . . figures for . . . . are
   EXCELLENT / ENCOURAGING / DISAPPOINTING / DISASTROUS.

6. The demand for . . . . in . . . . is
   ENORMOUS / CONSIDERABLE / GROWING / NEGLIGIBLE.

7. The service we get from . . . . is
   FIRST-CLASS / REASONABLE / UNSATISFACTORY / POOR.

8. Our . . . . supplier's prices are
   UNBEATABLE / COMPETITIVE / REASONABLE / EXCESSIVE.

TASK 2

Now find three adjectives above which could have these words in front of them:

fairly	. . . .	. . . .	. . . .
virtually	. . . .	. . . .	. . . .
extremely	. . . .	. . . .	. . . .
absolutely	. . . .	. . . .	. . . .

Business Terms 2

> Presenting is not just about giving information, but also about commenting on it. You need adjectives to comment on the main themes of your presentation.

TASK 1

Complete the following statements with information which is relevant to your work or company, by first filling in the gaps and then highlighting the most suitable positive or negative adjective or adding one of your own.

1. The future for . . . . is looking
   BRIGHT / PROMISING / UNCERTAIN / BLEAK.

2. The terms . . . . are offering us are
   GENEROUS / ATTRACTIVE / FAIR / UNACCEPTABLE.

3. The opportunities for . . . . in . . . . are
   EXCELLENT / GOOD / LIMITED / NON-EXISTENT.

4. The risks we face if we . . . . are
   NEGLIGIBLE / MINOR / SUBSTANTIAL / ENORMOUS.

5. Our negotiations with . . . . were
   SUCCESSFUL / PRODUCTIVE / INCONCLUSIVE / FRUITLESS.

6. The increase / decrease in . . . . has been
   DRAMATIC / RAPID / STEADY / GRADUAL.

7. The costs involved in . . . . will be
   INSIGNIFICANT / MODEST / CONSIDERABLE / PROHIBITIVE.

8. . . . . products are
   UNBEATABLE / UNCOMPETITIVE / UNPROFITABLE / UNMARKETABLE.

TASK 2

Now find three adjectives above which could have these words in front of them:

very	. . . .	. . . .	. . . .
relatively	. . . .	. . . .	. . . .
highly	. . . .	. . . .	. . . .
totally	. . . .	. . . .	. . . .

Business Terms 3

> The first step in preparing your presentation is to establish the key topics you want to deal with. This helps you to predict many of the words you may need.

TASK

Put the verbs and verb phrases in the word partnerships below into the *most likely* chronological order. Are there any alternative sequences?

1. AN ORDER   confirm   receive   dispatch   place   process

2. A COMPANY   sell off   set up   buy back   expand   put...on the market

3. A PROJECT   launch   axe   work on   instigate   jeopardize

4. A MEMBER OF STAFF   dismiss   headhunt   train   recruit   promote

5. A PROPOSAL   accept   put forward   implement   come up with   consider

Choose the keywords above which are more relevant to your job and expand the five stages into a short presentation.

88

Business Terms 4

> Many processes – price movements, product development etc. – describe a more or less fixed sequence of events. Make sure you know all the words you need to describe each stage in the processes you want to talk about.

TASK

Put the verbs and verb phrases in the word partnerships below into the *most likely* chronological order. Are there any alternative sequences?

1. THE MARKET   take over   target   be forced out of   re-enter   break into

2. NEGOTIATIONS   break off   complete   conduct   resume   enter into

3. PRICES   cut   set   re-think   raise   receive complaints about

4. THE CONTRACT   draw up   breach   negotiate   terminate   renew

5. THE PRODUCT   manufacture   distribute   launch   withdraw   develop

Choose the keywords above which are more relevant to your job and expand the five stages into a short presentation.

Business Terms 5

You should always look out for words you hear or read often in the context of your work. Learning these will give you the confidence to talk about your job fluently and precisely.

TASK

Put the verbs and verb phrases in the word partnerships below into the *most likely* chronological order. Are there any alternative sequences?

1. A PROBLEM solve suspect clarify tackle identify

2. LOSSES suffer write off forecast announce recover from

3. A COMMERCIAL run devise re-run update produce

4. RESEARCH abandon believe in carry out cut back on put money into

5. THE COMPETITION undercut identify outsell take on destroy

Choose the keywords above which are more relevant to your job and expand the five stages into a short presentation.

Business Terms 6

> Whenever you learn an important new word partnership, try to learn its opposite as well. eg. *to consider / to rule out* an option. Keep a record of those you could use in your own presentations to make dramatic contrasts.

Look at the pairs of verbs and verb expressions in the charts below. Which of the nouns in each list form strong word partnerships with both? The first one has been done for you as an example. Add a translation of a partnership, for example *to withdraw a proposal*.

VERB	OPPOSITE	NOUN	TRANSLATION

a proposal   a product   prices   matters   a budget   an opportunity

VERB	OPPOSITE	NOUN	TRANSLATION
1. put forward	withdraw	*a proposal*	
2. raise	drop		
3. seize	miss		
4. phase in	phase out		
5. stay within	exceed		
6. simplify	complicate		

costs   the competition   customers   an offer   a strategy   restrictions

VERB	OPPOSITE	NOUN	TRANSLATION
7. attract	put off		
8. bring down	push up		
9. impose	lift		
10. beat	lose out to		
11. accept	reject		
12. adopt	abandon		

a decision   capital   staff   a reputation   production   a deadline

VERB	OPPOSITE	NOUN	TRANSLATION
13. meet	miss		
14. raise	use up		
15. support	oppose		
16. take on	make redundant		
17. speed up	hold up		
18. build up	destroy		

Formality 1

In general, 'Latin' words *(affirm, conclude, demonstrate, discover)* suggest formality; shorter, often Germanic, words and phrasal verbs *(say, end, show, find out)* sound more conversational.

TASK

Match up the verbs on the left with a more formal alternative. Then match each pair of verbs with a phrase on the right to make a complete expression. The first example has been done for you.

WE REALLY NEED TO . . . .

1. set up	a. conduct	1. the problem of distribution.
2. carry out	b. investigate	2. a sister company in Hamburg.
3. strengthen	c. establish	3. our position in South America.
4. look into	d. consolidate	4. more research in this area.

5. buy	e. re-locate	1. the possibility of selling direct.
6. think about	f. purchase	2. our headquarters to Lyon.
7. move	g. amalgamate	3. our raw materials at source.
8. combine	h. explore	4. the two departments.

9. show	i. penetrate	1. the development of new product.
10. work out	j. accelerate	2. the importance of the project.
11. speed up	k. calculate	3. new markets in Eastern Europe.
12. break into	l. demonstrate	4. exactly what our margins are.

13. pay	m. collaborate	1. the goods within the month.
14. send	n. exploit	2. staff according to performance.
15. work together	o. remunerate	3. our cross-cultural expertise.
16. make use of	p. dispatch	4. on the design of the product.

17. use	q. formulate	1. all our resources.
18. build in	r. capitalize on	2. several new product features.
19. think up	s. incorporate	3. the new opportunities in the CIS.
20. take advantage of	t. utilize	4. an immediate plan of action.

How formal are the presentations you have to give or attend? Do you find an informal approach works best, even in a formal situation?

Formality 2

> In technical and scientific presentations, where processes and procedures
> are being described, it is common to use the passive:
>> **Each component** was tested **to destruction.**
>> **The first studies** were carried out **in Germany.**
>
> To sound less formal, use the active with *we* or *they:*
>> We tested **each component to destruction.**
>> They carried out **the first studies in Germany.**
>
> Unattributed facts and opinions certainly sound confident:
>> It's a well-known fact that **what the West researches the East develops.**
>> It's a little-known fact that **90% of all new products fail.**
>> It's a common misconception that **advertising works.**
>
> But the following generalizations sound more friendly:
>> **Everybody knows that** what the West researches the East develops.
>> **A lot of people don't realize that** 90% of all new products fail.
>> **People often make the mistake of thinking that** advertising works.

TASK

Using the words given, make these presentation extracts more informal:

1. It's a well-known fact that the Internet is the information channel of the future.
   (Everybody) . . . .

2. It's been proved that direct mailing gets a less than 1% response rate.
   (They) . . . .

3. It's being suggested that so-called smart drugs can actually increase intelligence.
   (They) . . . .

4. It's generally agreed that the number of new cases of AIDS is falling.
   (Almost everyone) . . . .

5. It's widely believed that Thailand and Malaysia will continue to outgrow Taiwan.
   (A lot / us) . . . .

6. It's not known whether a mile-high building is technically possible.
   (We / not know) . . . .

7. It's a little-known fact that more people die of tuberculosis every year than were
   killed in both world wars.
   (A lot / people / not realize) . . . .

8. It's a popular misconception that Total Quality originated in Japan.

   (People often / mistake / thinking) . . . .

9. It's debatable whether such an ambitious objective can be achieved in two years.
   (We can't / sure / we) . . . .

10. It's doubtful whether a cure for the common cold will ever be found.
    (We / not expect / anyone) . . . .

Remember, simple grammatical choices like these can affect the whole tone of your presentation.

Useful Expressions 1

> You can cut down the amount of thinking you have to do in a presentation by learning in advance some of the most common expressions you might need. Simple verbs like *make, do, give* and *take* are the basis of many of these.

`cass` **PRESENTATION**

Complete the following extracts from a presentation using the appropriate forms of *make, do, give* and *take*. Then use the frames to record the important word partnerships.

PART 1

First of all, I'd like to (a) . . . . this opportunity to welcome you all to our new plant here in Alfortville. In a few moments you'll be (b) . . . . on a tour of the main laboratories, which will (c) . . . . you a general overview of the research we're currently (d) . . . . and you'll be able to see some of the many improvements we've (e) . . . . to the IT unit. In each department you visit this morning there will be people on hand to answer any questions you may have and to help you (f) . . . . the most of your day with us.

WORD PARTNERSHIP	TRANSLATION

PART 2

Perhaps I could just (a) . . . . a few minutes to (b) . . . . you the background to the work we're (c) . . . . in the search for an AIDS vaccine, because this is an area where we're finally starting to (d) . . . . real progress. As you know, it (e) . . . . time to get a drug through pre-clinical trials, and it's far too early to say whether we've (f) . . . . .the major breakthrough we've all been hoping for. But what we have done is (g) . . . . an important step towards finding a preventive solution to AIDS.

WORD PARTNERSHIP	TRANSLATION

PART 3

I'd like to (a) . . . . a distinction here between what I call innovative and imitative research. Of course, it's the innovative companies who consistently (b) . . . . the lead in pharmaceutical research and (c). . . . . the biggest contribution to the development of new medicines. But let's not forget that improving existing drugs can (d) . . . . a difference, too. For one thing, it can make a prohibitively expensive drug affordable. It's easy to think that research is all about (e) . . . . initiatives, and (f) . . . . an impact on the world of science. But when research is your business, you can often (g) . . . . more damage to company profits by (h) . . . . a chance on something new and (i) . . . . a mess of it than by settling for (j) . . . . a good product better.

WORD PARTNERSHIP	TRANSLATION

PART 4

There's an important point that needs (a) . . . . here. While it's true that in terms of European over-the-counter sales we're (b) . . . . headway, in the Far East illegal copies of our drugs have (c) . . . . a real bite out of OTC profits. To (d) . . . . you some idea of the extent of the losses, you have only to (e) . . . . a comparison between projected and actual sales. We may have (f). . . . . a good job of protecting our patents in the West, but what action can you (g) . . . . against countries where the law virtually permits pharmaceutical piracy? Three years ago a survey was (h) . . . . and, as you might expect, China came out as the worst offender. Now, I don't want to (i) . . . . you the impression that the situation is hopeless, but I could (j) . . . . you hundreds of examples of Chinese copies of our bestselling drugs turning up all over the Far East. Believe me, we've really (k) . . . . our homework on this one, and China poses a serious commercial threat.

WORD PARTNERSHIP	TRANSLATION

Useful Expressions 2

English is full of useful fixed expressions which native speakers use all the time, almost without thinking. The ability to use some of these will make your talk sound more confident and idiomatic.

cass **PRESENTATION**

Complete the following extracts from a presentation using the appropriate forms of *go*, *take*, and *get*. In each extract the same verb will fill all the spaces, but different forms – *go*, *going*, *gone* – might be needed.

PART 1

OK, let's (a) . . . . down to business.

Three months ago we were well ahead of schedule on the Buenos Aires contract. Six weeks ago we'd fallen behind. Now it's (b) . . . . ridiculous! Work has virtually come to a complete halt. True, one of our suppliers let us down at the last minute. But, frankly, that's (c) . . . . nothing to do with it.

No, I'm afraid, there's no (d) . . . . away from it – we've (e) . . . . real problems here. So, let's stop wasting time. We need to (f) . . . . to the bottom of this as quickly as possible. After all, we (g) . . . . ourselves into this mess, so we ought to be able to (h) . . . . ourselves out of it . . . .

WORD PARTNERSHIP		TRANSLATION
get		

PART 2

So much for Argentina. We knew we were (a) . . . . a risk when we went over there and now it looks as though we'll just have to (b) . . . . the consequences.

Fortunately, I can report good progress in Sao Paulo. It has (c) . . . . a great deal of hard work, but it looks as though things are finally starting to (d) . . . . shape.

To be honest, we knew there was an undersupplied market in Brazil and we were quick to (e) . . . . advantage of the situation. It'll be a year or more before we see the real benefits, but we're in no hurry. These things (f) . . . . time. And you can (g) . . . . it from me, the medium-term prospects look very good indeed. You can expect things to really start (h) . . . . off within two years . . . .

WORD PARTNERSHIP		TRANSLATION
take		

PART 3

Finally, Santiago. Well, everything was (a) . . . . fine until last quarter. But, as you know, that's when things started to (b) . . . . wrong. And, to be honest, since then things have just (c) . . . . from bad to worse.

Obviously, we've done everything we can to put things right. That (d) . . . . without saying. But there's still a long way to (e) . . . . It could take six months to get things running properly again.

Anyway, there's no (f) . . . . back now. And if we can get our act together, we might just manage it. So, I say, let's (g) . . . . for it! What have we got to lose?

WORD PARTNERSHIP		TRANSLATION
go		

Useful Expressions 3

> Most of the arguments you put forward in a presentation depend on several
> factors eg. time, money, manpower, the competition, the state of the market.
> **Sentence qualifiers** are short phrases:
>
> > **in theory   on average   up to a point**
>
> They put the rest of what you say into context.

TASK 1

**Match the pairs of statements below and add *in, at, on, as* and *up*. The first one has been
done for you as an example.**

1. In theory, there's always a market for quality.

2. Forget about the number of unsold units.

3. Why don't we sell the system in Mexico?

4. It's not easy doing business in Kuwait.

5. It's time to start thinking about advertising.

a. . . . . least we know there's a market
for it there.

b. . . . . average, everything takes three
times longer than it does here.

c . . . . to now we've been lucky – the
product has virtually sold itself.

d. . . . . a last resort, we can always sell
them at cost.

e. In practice, people want low prices.

Now complete the sentence qualifiers:

in	. . . .	as	. . . .
at	. . . .	up	. . . .
on	. . . .		

TASK 2

1. We need to rethink the whole project.

2. The recession hasn't harmed us at all.

3. Direct selling has proved ineffective.

4. Let's look at the problem of data security.

5. We propose to downsize all departments.

a. . . . . things stand, our system is only
as safe as the person operating it.

b. . . . . to a point, it's been a success, but
there's still room for improvement.

c. . . . . the contrary, we've actually
benefited from it.

d. . . . . present, staffing levels are
unacceptably high.

e. . . . . general, mailshots just don't
work.

in	. . . .	as	. . . .
at	. . . .	up	. . . .
on	. . . .		

TASK 3

1. The market situation's not all bad news.

2. We enjoy tremendous customer loyalty.

3. We started to run into difficulties last year.

4. We don't have a product visibility problem.

5. Major re-investment is not necessary.

a. . . . . the most, we'll have to upgrade the hardware we've already got.

b. . . . . the whole, brand recognition was high in the survey we carried out.

c. . . . . some respects we've actually improved our position.

d. . . . . a direct result, we've had three years of sustained growth.

e. . . . . until then everything was fine.

in	. . . .	as	. . . .
at	. . . .	up	. . . .
on	. . . .		

PRESENTATION

In the spaces below write pairs of statements relevant to your own work, company or interests, using the context expressions given. Don't just write anything. Think of points you might actually want to make in a presentation.

FIRST POINT	FOLLOW-UP POINT
1.	In general, ...
2.	On average, ...
3.	At least, ...
4.	Up to now, ...
5.	On the whole, ...
6.	At present, ...
7.	On the contrary, ...
8.	In some respects, ...
9. In theory, ...	In practice, ...
10.	As a last resort, ...

Useful Expressions 4

> Short phrases *(in effect, on the other hand, at a guess)* help you to qualify your arguments and organize your presentation better. Learn these by heart, so that you can use them when you need them.

TASK 1

Match the pairs of statements below and add *in, at, on, as* and *under*. The first one has been done for you as an example.

1. The company's worth no more than $75m.

2. Interest rates aren't coming down.

3. Productivity is up by over 85%.

4. The Scottish plant is simply inefficient.

5. Growth in Eastern Europe will be slow.

a. . . . . a matter of fact, they're still on the increase.

b. . . . . the circumstances, we have no option but to close it down.

c. . . . . any rate, that's what the banks are saying.

d. **On** no account should we pay the asking price of a hundred.

e. . . . . effect, output has almost doubled.

in	. . . .	as	. . . .
at	. . . .	under	. . . .
on	. . . .		

TASK 2

1. It'll take time to win any business in Tokyo.

2. Profits are not looking good.

3. Yes, we do need to keep prices down.

4. Production's been halted for the time being.

5. Low profits in Spain aren't a major concern.

a. . . . . the face of it, this seems to make sense, but it does mean lay-offs.

b. . . . . a general rule, the Japanese like to get to know you first.

c. . . . . any case, they're more than offset by the gains we've made in Italy.

d. . . . . no circumstances, though, should we get ourselves into a price war.

e. . . . . best, they might reach 9 million.

in	. . . .	as	. . . .
at	. . . .	under	. . . .
on	. . . .		

TASK 3

1. We've heard nothing now for over a month.	a. . . . . first glance, they look pretty good, but there are hidden costs.
2. Is a joint venture a good idea?	b. . . . . the other hand, turnover is slightly down.
3. On the one hand, sales are up on last year.	c. . . . . other words, it looks like the deal's off.
4. Here are the prices we've been quoted.	d. . . . . the right conditions we should be able to do the same in Germany.
5. We've always made money in the UK.	e. . . . . far as we're concerned, no.

in	. . . .	as	. . . .
at	. . . .	under	. . . .
on	. . . .		

PRESENTATION

In the spaces below write pairs of statements relevant to your own work, company or interests, using the context expressions given. Don't just write anything. Think of points you might actually want to make in a presentation.

FIRST POINT	FOLLOW-UP POINT
1.	At first glance, ...
. . . .	. . . .
2.	As a matter of fact, ...
. . . .	. . . .
3.	In any case, ...
. . . .	. . . .
4. On the one hand, ...	On the other hand, ...
. . . .	. . . .
5.	On no account, ...
. . . .	. . . .
6.	As a general rule, ...
. . . .	. . . .
7.	In any case, ...
. . . .	. . . .
8.	At best, ...
. . . .	. . . .
9. Yes, ...	But under no circumstances, ...
. . . .	. . . .
10. It's true that	But as far as we're concerned, ...
. . . .	. . . .

Say the above several times until you are happy with the way you sound.

Useful Expressions 5

More important than the expressions which you have been presented with in this section are those which you yourself find and decide will be useful in your situation.

USEFUL EXPRESSION	TRANSLATION

Handling Questions

How to deal with questions from the audience, both friendly and hostile

"IS IT WORKING NOW?"

Clarification 1

> When you give a presentation in English, one of your main objectives is to sound clear. But when there are misunderstandings, a small audience should be prepared to interrupt you to clarify what you said.

TASK 1

Here are four simple ways of checking with the presenter. Write in the missing pairs of words.

follow + run   missed + say   see + explain   catch + repeat

You didn't hear:

1. Sorry, I . . . . that. Could you . . . . that again, please?
2. Sorry, I didn't . . . . that. Could you . . . . it, please?

You don't understand:

3. Sorry, I don't quite . . . . you. Could you just . . . . through that again, please?
4. Sorry, I don't quite . . . . what you mean. Could you just . . . . that, please?

TASK 2

Sometimes it is not enough to tell the speaker you don't understand. You need to say exactly what you don't understand. In these examples how do the questioners make it clear which points they missed?

Presenter	Questioner
1. Turnover was ▓▓▓▓	Sorry, turnover was **what?**
2. The greatest demand was in ▓▓▓▓	Sorry, the greatest demand was **where?**
3. We contacted ▓▓▓▓ in Tokyo.	Sorry, you contacted **who?**
4. We finished the study last ▓▓▓▓	Sorry, you finished the study **when?**
5. The whole project needs ▓▓▓▓	Sorry, the whole project needs **what?**
6. Our main market is in ▓▓▓▓	Sorry, our main market is **where?**
7. We've known this since ▓▓▓▓	Sorry, you've known this since **when?**
8. Start-up costs could be ▓▓▓▓	Sorry, start-up costs could be **how much?**
9. The study took ▓▓▓▓ to complete.	Sorry, the study took **how long** to complete?
10. We've had ▓▓▓▓ of enquiries.	Sorry, you've had **how many** enquiries?

TASK 3

Now you try these. If you are in a group, work with a partner. Take turns to be the questioner and interrupt the presenter. If you are working alone, listen to your cassette and interrupt to ask for clarification

1. Presenter: This is not the time to be thinking of ▓▓▓▓▓▓ **(expansion)**

   Questioner: . . . .

2. Presenter: We need to think about exporting to ▓▓▓▓▓▓ **(Spain)**

   Questioner: . . . .

3. Presenter: Clearly, the best person is ▓▓▓▓▓▓ **(Mr Branson)**

   Questioner: . . . .

4. Presenter: The market leaders are ▓▓▓▓▓▓ **(the French)**

   Questioner: . . . .

5. Presenter: We must reach our preliminary target by ▓▓▓▓▓▓ **(October)**

   Questioner: . . . .

6. Presenter: The main problem, of course, is going to be ▓▓▓▓▓▓ **(money)**

   Questioner: . . . .

7. Presenter: Advertising has cost us well over ▓▓▓▓▓▓ **(half a million)**

   Questioner: . . . .

8. Presenter: Do we pull out now? The answer is ▓▓▓▓▓▓ **(No)**

   Questioner: . . . .

9. Presenter: As a market, Brazil is very different from ▓▓▓▓▓▓ **(Argentina)**

   Questioner: . . . .

10. Presenter: We need to be putting more money into ▓▓▓▓▓▓ **(R&D)**

    Questioner: . . . .

11. Presenter: We should know the results by ▓▓▓▓▓▓ **(the end of the year)**

    Questioner: . . . .

12. Presenter: We've been forced to cut prices by ▓▓▓▓▓▓ **(30%)**

    Questioner: . . . .

13. Presenter: It might take ▓▓▓▓▓▓ to finalize the details. **(months)**

    Questioner: . . . .

14. Presenter: There are more than ▓▓▓▓▓▓ similar products on the market. **(fifty)**

    Questioner: . . . .

105

Clarification 2

> In an informal presentation being able to interrupt a speaker politely and effectively to ask for clarification is an important professional skill.

cass **TASK**

Read the following presentation extract and listen to it on your cassette. Some of the information is unclear. After each unclear piece of information you have a few seconds to ask for clarification. Then the presenter will answer you. Repeat this activity with and without the text until you can do it easily.

1. I'd like to spend a minute or two looking at the ▆▆▆▆▆▆ in Eastern Europe.

2. You'll find detailed figures in the report in front of you, together with our projections to the year ▆▆▆▆▆▆ .

3. If you read section 1 of the report, you'll find that the Czech Republic and Poland come out on top and are actually expected to be amongst Europe's fastest growing economies over the next ▆▆▆▆▆▆ .

4. In fact, the Czech Republic's credit rating is a healthy ▆▆▆▆▆▆ .

5. That's partly because they managed to pay off their entire IMF debt two years ahead of schedule in ▆▆▆▆▆▆ .

6. Quite an achievement when you consider that the debt once stood at around ▆▆▆▆▆▆ dollars.

7. OK, what about Poland? Well, we're expecting them to perform almost as well as the Czech Republic, with about four or five percent ▆▆▆▆▆▆ . Maybe more.

8. The problem in Poland, of course, is ▆▆▆▆▆▆ .

9. And unless it can be kept below ▆▆▆▆▆▆ , the outlook is not so good.

10. Now, the ▆▆▆▆▆▆ , of course, were economic reformists even under communism.

11. So you'd probably expect them to be doing well. But in fact, Hungary's growth rate is rather ▆▆▆▆▆▆ .

12. Especially when you consider the amount of foreign ▆▆▆▆▆▆ that has poured into Hungary since the collapse of the Soviet Union.

13. For instance, do you know how much money was invested in the former Soviet bloc between 1990 and 1994? ▆▆▆▆▆▆ dollars!

14. And guess how much of that went to Hungary? Almost ▆▆▆▆▆▆ .

PRESENTATION

STEP 1

Think of a subject you know quite a lot about but your study partners don't. It could be something to do with your job or a personal interest. The more complicated or technical the subject is, the better! Spend 15-20 minutes preparing a 5-minute talk on this subject. Just write down the main points.

SUBJECT OF TALK	
MAIN POINTS	1. . . . .
	2. . . . .
	3. . . . .
	4. . . . .
	5. . . . .

STEP 2

Tell your partners what the subject of your talk is. Tell them that at the end you will ask one of them to stand up and accurately summarize what you said. But don't tell them who you are going to ask. (If you are working with just one partner, tell them you will test them on your subject at the end of your talk.)

STEP 3

Give your talk. Make sure you speak for at least 5 minutes. Speak as fast as you can and imagine that you are talking to a group of experts in your subject. Don't worry about your grammar, your vocabulary or your pronunciation. Just keep talking! Your partners should interrupt you as often as necessary to check they understand.

STEP 4

Choose one of your partners to summarize what you talked about. If they can't, invite them to ask you as many questions as they need to so that they can.

NOTE

If you are working alone, record yourself giving the talk. Then play back the recording, pause the cassette at the end of each sentence and ask a clarifying question.

Clarification 3

A large audience may not get the chance to ask questions until the presenter has finished the talk. So, if you want to clarify something the presenter said, first focus their attention on the subject you are unclear about:

1. Focus   **You talked about concentrating on our core business.**
2. Clarification   **Could you say a bit more about that?**

In a longer presentation you may need to contextualize your question more:

1. Context   **When you were talking about raising capital, . . .**
2. Focus   **. . . you mentioned the possibility of a flotation.**
3. Clarification   **Could you clarify your position on that?**

cass **TASK**

Below you will find the requests for clarification which followed a presentation about foreign investment in China. Complete them using appropriate verbs from the lists. Combining the three parts of number 1 will give you a complete question. Then do the same with numbers 2, 3, 4, and 5.

WHEN YOU WERE . . . .

dealing   talking   telling   describing   showing   summing up

1. . . . . about the current level of foreign investment in China, ...

2. . . . . to us what kind of future you see for China, ...

3. . . . . with the issue of China's communist administration, ...

4. . . . . China's economic prospects over the next five years, ...

5. . . . . us China's trade figures for the last three years, ...

6. . . . . us why there's so much interest at the moment in Asian-Pacific markets, ...

YOU . . . .

commented   spoke   referred   quoted   made   said

1. . . . . a figure of $34 billion.

2. . . . . on the importance of Hong Kong.

3. . . . . the point that they had created a free market within a command economy.

4. . . . . something about hundreds of billions of dollars still being needed.

5. . . . . about private enterprise gradually taking over from state ownership.

6. . . . . to a decline in foreign investment elsewhere, particularly in Latin America.

108

COULD YOU . . . .

explain   run   be   tell   elaborate   say

1. . . . . us how you arrived at that figure?

2. . . . . a bit more about that?

3. . . . . to us exactly what you meant by that?

4. . . . . a little more specific?

5. . . . . on that?

6. . . . . us through that again?

Now highlight all the useful expressions above, eg. *talking about, dealing with etc.*

PRESENTATION

1. Record yourself giving a short talk on a specialist subject (3-5mins).
2. Swap cassette recordings with your study partners and prepare a set of clarifying questions to ask each other. The following question frames may help you.
3. Record the question-and-answer sessions.

---

1. What exactly did you mean by . . . . ?

2. Could we go back to what you were saying about . . . . ?

3. How did you arrive at the figure of . . . . ?

4. I think I misunderstood you. Did you say . . . . ?

5. You spoke about . . . . Could you explain that in more detail?

6. Going back to the question of . . . . Can you be more specific?

7. You didn't mention . . . . Why not?

8. If I understood you correctly, ... Is that right?

9. I'm not sure I fully understood . . . . Can you run through that again, please?

10. There's one thing I'm not clear about: . . . . Could you go over that again, please?

NOTE

If you are working alone, play back the recording of your talk and write down some of the questions you would expect an audience of experts to ask you, using the question frames above to help you.

Dealing with Questions 1

When someone in the audience asks you a question, it's a good idea to comment on it before you actually answer it. This gives you time to think. There are four basic types of question:

Good questions
Thank people for asking them. They help you to get your message across to the audience better.

Difficult questions
These are the ones you can't or prefer not to answer. Say you don't know, offer to find out or ask the questioner what they think.

Unnecessary questions
You have already given this information. Point this out, answer briefly again and move on.

Irrelevant questions
Try not to sound rude, but move on.

TASK

Put the following responses into 4 groups: responses to good questions, difficult questions, unnecessary questions and irrelevant questions.

1. I'm afraid I don't see the connection.
2. Sorry, I don't follow you.
3. I don't know that off the top of my head.
4. Can I get back to you on that?
5. I think I answered that earlier.
6. Good point.
7. Interesting. What do you think?
8. Well, as I said . . .
9. I'm afraid I'm not in a position to comment on that.
10. I wish I knew.
11. I'm glad you asked that.
12. Well, as I mentioned earlier, . . .
13. To be honest, I think that raises a different issue.
14. That's a very good question.
15. I'm afraid I don't have that information with me.

GOOD	DIFFICULT	UNNECESSARY	IRRELEVANT

Repeat the phrases until you feel comfortable saying them. Choose one or two you like from each category.

Dealing with Questions 2

> When people ask you questions, listen carefully. Avoid the temptation to interrupt. Take a moment to think about and then comment on each question before you actually answer it.

cass TASK

Read and / or listen to the following presentation extract. Imagine that you are going to give this presentation. You want to be prepared for any question which may come from the audience. Make a list of possible questions and think up what you would say in reply. There are suggestions in the answer key to this unit.

I think it would be true to say that throughout the late 1970s and early 80s our company was the classic American success story. We started from nothing and we built a billion-dollar business on product innovation. We enjoyed a virtual monopoly. No-one could touch us. We were the defining force in an industry which, for almost fifteen years, we dominated.

But by the mid 80s we had begun to lose our way. First, we lost a large slice of our business to Rand Reprographics, the Canadian start-up which grew into a major competitor almost overnight. That came as a shock. And second, we found ourselves facing some very stiff competition from Japan. It's an indication of just how much we'd lost touch with the market that we didn't even realize the sheer scale of the Japanese threat until it was almost too late. In one year, 1989, our earnings were slashed by more than 60%. We'd hit rock-bottom.

But 1990 was the year in which a new corporate strategy began to unfold, as we reinvented ourselves to become a total quality company. And over the next three years manufacturing costs were cut in half; supply lines cut back to a minimum; product development cycles pushed to the limits. The improvements were modest at first. And nobody expected us to make a full recovery. But, little by little, since 1992 we've won back three-quarters of the market share we lost.

PRESENTATION

1. Prepare a short talk on a topic of your choice. Don't choose anything too technical unless your study partners know the subject well.

2. Tell your study partners what you are going to talk about and let them see the notes you made while you were preparing.

3. In pairs or small groups, your study partners should prepare different types of question to ask you. One group should prepare a set of irrelevant questions on subjects not directly connected with your talk. Another group should prepare a set of the most difficult questions they can think of – precise figures, for example. A third group should prepare a set of interesting or controversial questions related to your subject.

4. Give your talk. The others will interrupt you to ask their questions. Your teacher may also interrupt you to ask you questions you have already answered! Deal with each type of question as politely as you can – even the stupid ones!

Dealing with Questions 3

The exchange of questions and answers at the end of your presentation is something you need to prepare for. Simple questions can be easily answered. But the answers to more complex questions are often negotiated between the presenter and the questioner.

cass TASK

A financial analyst has just given a presentation to a group of international bankers on the prospects for ten key industrial sectors. Here is the question-and-answer session that followed her presentation. Put the following exchanges in the right order and highlight useful expressions. The first expression is always the first.

EXCHANGE 1   Inviting Questions

1. Are there any questions you'd like to ask?

2. Well, obviously the airlines would be one; telecommunications probably another.

3. Could I ask you which industries this is most likely to affect?

4. That's right, we see that as a general trend over the next five years.

5. Yes, I have a question. You spoke about increased deregulation and privatization.

The correct order is ____ ____ ____ ____ ____

The cassette provides a good model for you. Use it to check your answers after you have done the exercise.

EXCHANGE 2   Querying a Point

1. When you were looking at the agricultural sector, you mentioned Japan.

2. Quite. Did you say there might be some relaxation of the restrictions on imports?

3. Well, considering the way the GATT talks went, that's good news.

4. Yes, it's difficult not to mention Japan in the context of agriculture.

5. I did. Japanese farmers are not the political force they were. Restrictions could go.

The correct order is ____ ____ ____ ____ ____

EXCHANGE 3   Asking for Additional Information

1. While we're on the subject of Japan, who would you say are the companies to watch?

2. Which is, no doubt, why so many Japanese car makers have set up factories there.

3. Good question. Certainly not the computer companies and the car manufacturers.

4. Well, the fact is, their capacity's being severely cut as pressure mounts from Europe.

5. Computer companies, I can understand, but why not the car companies?

> The correct order is ____ ____ ____ ____ ____

EXCHANGE 4   Referring to an Earlier Point

1. Going back to what you were saying about the German car components industry, ...

2. Yes, and from Western countries like Spain and Britain too.

3. Ah yes, I thought someone might pick me up on that.

4. I see. So it looks as though a lot of German components firms could go under.

5. You suggested it was in decline. Competition from Eastern Europe, I suppose?

> The correct order is ____ ____ ____ ____ ____

EXCHANGE 5   Making a Criticism

1. I want to take you up on what you said about Asia being a high growth area.

2. No, not really. Surely this Asian boom is just the result of low pay and long hours?

3. Even so, I still think you've exaggerated its short-term potential.

4. You're not convinced?

5. Not at all, it's actually a result of great improvements in education and infrastructure.

> The correct order is ____ ____ ____ ____ ____

Dealing with Questions 4

It sometimes seems as if the person asking the questions has all the power. But try to remember that, by giving your presentation, you have set the agenda.

`cass` **TASK**

Put these exchanges in the right order. Highlight any useful expressions.

EXCHANGE 1   Pushing for an Answer

1. What kind of a future, if any, do you see for European electrical consumer goods?

2. Yes, that's all very well, but what I want to know is, can they become competitive?

3. So, what you're saying is, the future of the industry in Europe depends on the yen.

4. Competitive? It's difficult to say. If the yen continues to be strong, it'll obviously push up the price of imported Japanese goods, and that'll help.

5. Well, with cost cutting and decentralization, they should, at least, stop losing money.

The correct order is ____ ____ ____ ____ ____

EXCHANGE 2   Asking for Proof

1. On what basis do you forecast a future for oil? Surely, gas is the fuel of the future.

2. Sure. Right now in the Gulf of Mexico oil is being pumped at incredible depths.

3. Well, I'm not so sure. Can you give us an example of this new technology at work?

4. Mm. That may be so. But I still think there are limits to what technology can do.

5. Only in Europe. New technology is going to extend the life of many of the world's oil fields.

The correct order is ____ ____ ____ ____ ____

EXCHANGE 3   Rephrasing a Question

1. You mentioned the construction of power stations in Asia. Can you expand on that?

2. Oh, I see. So what you're asking is how many Asian countries will go nuclear?

3. No, I mean will countries like Thailand be looking for alternatives to coal and gas?

4. Do you mean, when do I expect them to be built?

5. Yes, that's what I'm asking.

> **The correct order is** ____ ____ ____ ____ ____

EXCHANGE 4   Voicing Concern

1. Just one thing worries me about investing in the French advertising industry.

2. So you said. But the growth in the number of European TV stations isn't going to make all that much difference, surely.

3. I understand your concern. But let me reassure you that the prospects are still good.

4. And what's that? The ban on tobacco advertising?

5. Well, yes. I mean it's cost the industry billions already.

> **The correct order is** ____ ____ ____ ____ ____

EXCHANGE 5   Accepting a Compliment

1. Can I just say that I thought your analysis of the media business was excellent.

2. Yes, as I said, the problem with satellite is that you can't regulate what is transmitted, and that obviously won't be popular in Islamic countries.

3. And with sixty million homes on cable by 2005, I'm sure that's the area to invest in.

4. And I totally agree with what you said about cable outselling satellite TV, especially in the Middle East.

5. Well, thank you very much. It's certainly an interesting area.

> **The correct order is** ____ ____ ____ ____ ____

Dealing with Questions 5

Try to see the question-and-answer session at the end of your presentation as an opportunity to relax and share more of your ideas with your audience.

cass **TASK**

Put these exchanges in the right order. Highlight useful expressions.

EXCHANGE 1   Avoiding an Answer

1. Do you agree that, with low interest rates and fierce competition from building societies, British banks are going to have a fight on their hands?

2. Of course, but I think you'd do better to ask one of the people sitting next to you.

3. Maybe not. But I'm sure you have an opinion on the matter.

4. Well, to be honest, I'm not really the right person to ask about that.

5. OK. Point taken. Perhaps we can talk about it later.

The correct order is ____ ____ ____ ____ ____

EXCHANGE 2   Conceding a Point

1. Wouldn't you agree that in pharmaceuticals R&D spending is coming under increasing pressure?

2. Right, I see what you're getting at. And, of course only one percent of those that do make it to market ever recover their R&D costs.

3. But surely you realize that only a tiny fraction of patented drugs ever make it to market. About one in five thousand, in fact.

4. Yes, but to some extent strategic alliances between companies compensate for that.

5. Exactly.

The correct order is ____ ____ ____ ____ ____

116

EXCHANGE 3   Dealing with Hostility

1. Do you really expect us to believe that big insurance companies are on the way out?

2. Yes, yes, but you still haven't answered my question!

3. Frankly, yes. New laws have been passed. And the EC is very keen on deregulation.

4. Nonsense! It's the little telesales companies that have given insurance a bad name.

5. Sorry, could I just finish? Deregulation means the smaller companies will benefit most.

The correct order is ____ ____ ____ ____ ____

EXCHANGE 4   Clearing up a Misunderstanding

1. If I understood you correctly, you said the computer industry had burned itself out.

2. Don't get me wrong. Innovation will continue, but a surplus of products clearly can't.

3. OK, fair enough. I see what you mean.

4. No, perhaps I didn't make myself clear. What I was trying to say was the rate of new product launches will have to slow down.

5. How do you mean? Product innovation is what the computer industry is all about.

The correct order is ____ ____ ____ ____ ____

EXCHANGE 5   Winding up the Question Session

1. Are there any more questions?

2. Right, if there are no other questions, perhaps we should wrap it up here. Thank you.

3. Of course. I think we all agree the Asia-Pacific region is the one to look at. Thanks.

4. Yes, I do. Particularly in the developing countries in the Far East.

5. Just one. Can I ask you if you expect to see an increase in cross-border investment?

The correct order is ____ ____ ____ ____ ____

Dealing with Questions 6

One thing all presenters worry about is hostile questions on difficult subjects. It's a particular problem when you're presenting in a meeting. In this situation it's best to be diplomatic but firm. You can disagree strongly, but try to avoid saying 'No'. Keep your answers short and simple. If necessary, be vague.

TASK

Complete the following exchanges by writing in the appropriate expressions:

EXCHANGE 1

Hopefully not   To some extent   True   Not yet

1. Have you reached an agreement on the Saudi contract yet?
   . . . . There are still one or two things we need to discuss.

2. But you've had six months to discuss them already.
   . . . . Six months does seem like a long time, but Arabs are very cautious.

3. Mm. Hasn't the fact that ours is the cheapest tender helped at all?
   . . . . But they'd like the first construction phase completed by July.

4. July! But then that's going to create all kinds of problems.
   . . . . We've rescheduled things and it might just be possible.

EXCHANGE 2

Yes, I know   Not quite   Not as a rule   Not necessarily

1. So, we lost all record of our accounts when the network went down, did we?
   . . . . Just the last six months.

2. I see. I suppose it's too late to do anything about it now?
   . . . . There might still be a way of getting into some of the files.

3. What I don't understand is why the accounts department didn't back up the system.
   . . . . That is the standard procedure.

4. Does this kind of thing happen a lot?
   . . . . It was just one of those things.

EXCHANGE 3

Granted   Not really   Not at all   Not entirely

1. You have to admit, the people in marketing have really made a mess of this launch.
   . . . . They've done a good job. It was a difficult brief.

2. But wouldn't it have been a good idea to get an agency in to do the creative work?
   . . . . For one thing, it would have cost considerably more.

3. But it was you who said we should be spending more on promotions.

. . . . But we just don't have the budget for that right now.

4. So, you're happy with the way the launch went, then?

. . . . But I think it went pretty well, given the circumstances.

EXCHANGE 4

It depends.　　Yes and no.　　On the whole, yes.　　Not if we can help it.

1. So, it's going to be another year of cuts, then?
. . . . There will be cuts, but an upgrade in lab facilities is long overdue.

2. Won't we need to get authorization for that?
. . . . Only if we exceed our budget.

3. But we will exceed it, won't we?
. . . . We've costed the whole thing pretty accurately.

4. But the facilities we already have are quite adequate, aren't they?
. . . . But that doesn't mean there aren't areas where we can't improve.

PRESENTATION

Are you trying to inform, sell something or persuade your audience to do something? Your purpose affects the kind of questions they might ask you. Prepare a set of questions which someone might ask. Use the questions below. Get someone to ask you the questions.

INFORMATIVE TALK
Could you expand on what you said about . . . . ?
Where did you get your information on . . . . ?
Are you in a position to tell us whether . . . . ?
Do you have (precise) figures for . . . . ?
Can you tell us how you arrived at the figure of . . . . ?

SALES TALK
How do / does your . . . . compare with . . . . in terms of . . . . ?
Suppose we said . . . . , would it be possible to . . . . ?
How flexible are you on . . . . ?
Could we rely on you to . . . . ?
What immediate / long-term benefits could we expect to see . . . . ?
What experience do you have of . . . . ?

PERSUASIVE TALK
What (real) evidence is there that . . . . ?
How can you be (so) sure that . . . . ?
How do we know that . . . . ?
I'm not (really) convinced that . . . .
How do you justify . . . . ?
I'd like to take you up on what you said about . . . .
Do you (honestly) expect us to believe that . . . . ?

If you add the word in brackets it makes the question more hostile.

Sometimes small variations are possible in the answers to a task. Discuss these with your teacher or a native speaker.

1.2 Stating Your Purpose 1

1. talking 2. telling 3. showing 4. taking 5. reporting

1. filling 2. making 3. outlining 4. giving 5. bringing

1. highlight 2. put 3. talk 4. make 5. discuss

1.3 Stating Your Purpose 2

2. stressing 3. putting forward 4. dealing with 5. raising 6. looking at 7. focus 8. sets out 9. suggesting
10. turn 11. spell out 12. address 13. get across 14. underline 15. come to

1.4 Effective Openings

Problems: 2, 6, 8 Amazing Facts: 1, 3, 5, 7 Stories: 4, 9

1.5 Signposting

Task 1 1. to move on (to your next point) 2. to turn to (last year's figures) 3. to go back (to what I said earlier)
4. to recap (on the main features of the SR125) 5. to expand on (this a bit more) 6. to elaborate on (this particular feature) 7. to summarize (the salient points) 8. to digress (just for a moment) 9. to conclude

Task 2 1. To summarize 2. To conclude 3. To elaborate (on) 4. To expand (on) 5. To recap (on)
6. To go back (to) 7. To move on 8. To digress 9. To turn to

Task 3 2. To expand on the figures for last year. 3. I'd like to recap on the main points. 4. Let's go back to the question of clinical research methods. 5. To digress for a moment, let's consider the alternatives. 6. Going back for a moment to the situation last year, 7. Let's turn now to our targets for the next five years. 8. I'd like to turn now to our projections to the year 2005. 9. To go back to the main reason for our collaboration with the Germans, 10. I'd like to expand on that a little before we move on. 11. Let's go back for a moment to what we were discussing earlier. 12. Let me expand on some of the main points in our proposal. 13. To elaborate on that a little for those of you who aren't familiar with Russian business practices, 14. If I could just move on to some of the problems we face in Central and Latin America, 15. I'd like to conclude, if I may, by repeating what I said at the beginning of this presentation.

1.6 Survival Tactics

Task 1 1. c 2. a 3. d 4. b 5. h 6. g 7. f 8. e

Task 2 1. Sorry, what I meant is this 2. So, let's just recap on that. 3. Sorry, I should just mention one thing. 4. So, basically what I'm saying is this 5. Sorry, perhaps I didn't make that quite clear. 6. Sorry, what's the word I'm looking for? 7. Sorry, let me rephrase that. 8. So, just to give you the main points here,

2.1 Introducing Visuals

Task 1 Graphs: 1, 7 Charts: 2 (pie chart), 4 (flowchart), 8, 9, 11 (table) Diagrams: 5, 6, 12
Note that 3 and 10 are (bar) graphs in American English and (bar) charts in British English.

Task 2 Extract 1: Have / Take a look at this graph. As you can see, it's a fairly typical growth curve for a young company in the early stages of its development. The vertical axis shows turnover in millions of dollars and the horizontal axis represents the years 1990 to 1996. **Extract 2:** The graph we're looking at very clearly demonstrates the comparative productivity of our European plants, and gives you some idea of how far production levels in the Netherlands, shown here, exceed the rest. **Extract 3:** I'd like you to look at this chart, which shows the current position of six of our leading products. Let's take a closer look for a moment at product movement in the high growth sector.

2.2 Commenting on Visuals

Task 1 1. at 2. on 3. about 4. out 5. to **Task 2** 1. As 2. If 3. However 4. Whatever 5. Whichever

Task 3 1. conclusions 2. lesson 3. implications 4. significance 5. message

2.3 Change and Development 1

Task 1 1. increase 2. rise 3. decrease 4. fall 5. shoot up 6. take off 7. plunge 8. slump 9. fluctuate 10. recover

11. pick up 12. stabilize 13. level off 14. remain steady 15. peak 16. hit a low 17. bottom out 18. grow
19. expand 20. shrink 21. decline

Task 2 1. fall-fell-fallen, shoot-shot-shot up, take-took-taken off, hit-hit-hit a low, grow-grew-grown, shrink-shrank-shrunk 2. an increase, a rise, a decrease, a fall, a plunge, a slump, a peak, a decline 3. recover - recovery, stabilize - stabilization, grow - growth, expand - expansion, shrink - shrinkage

Note: Some of the words in this exercise are strongly negative or positive. For example, you cannot say inflation slumped because slump is a negative word and a fall in inflation is a good thing. You would have to say inflation fell dramatically. In the same way, you cannot say taxes recovered because recover is a positive word and a rise in taxes is a bad thing. You would have to say taxes increased again.

2.4 Change and Development 2

Task 1 1. enormous 2. substantial 3. moderate 4. slight 5. rapid 6. steady 7. spectacular 8. encouraging
9. disappointing 10. disastrous

a. enormous, spectacular b. steady c. substantial, encouraging d. enormous, spectacular

Task 2 1. disappointingly 2. keenly 3. moderately 4. gradually

1. There was a slight / steady / tremendous increase in demand. 2. There was a sharp / considerable / marginal rise in interest rates. 3. There was a disastrous / sudden / rapid slump in profitability. 4. There was an enormous / a wild / a dramatic fluctuation in the price of oil.

2.5 Change and Development 3

Part 1 1. downs 2. upward 3. at 4. around 5. of 6. so **Part 2** 1. from 2. over 3. to 4. about 5. at 6. of
Part 3 1. downward 2. by 3. of 4. between 5. over 6. down **Part 4** 1 up 2. for 3. below 4. near 5. down 6. in
Task 2 1. ups 2. some 3. take 4. short 5. best 6. trend 7. dip 8. region 9. later 10. on

2.6 Cause, Effect and Purpose

Task 1 1. The launch was covered on TV and customer response rate increased significantly. 2. Operating costs have fallen dramatically because of last year's efforts. 3. We may need to modify the product to remain internationally competitive. 4. We successfully entered the market because our pricing strategy was competitive.
5. We increased investment to take advantage of the upturn in the economy. 6. Growth slowed down because we lost corporate confidence.

Task 2 Cause (because...): thanks to, can be traced back to, owing to, is attributable to Effect (and...): brought about, gave rise to, accounts for, resulted in

3.1 Articulation 1

Task 1 2. collaboration 3. negotiation 4. recommendation 5. decision 6. expansion
7. supervision 8. technician 9. politician 10. optional 11. provisional 12. unconditional

Task 2 1. strategic 2. dynamic 3. systematic 4. problematic 5. bureaucratic 6. typical 7. analytical
8. economical

Task 3 1. efficient 2. deficient 3. sufficient 4. proficient 5. experience 6. inconvenience 7. efficiency
8. deficiency

Task 4 1. essential 2. potential 3. beneficial 4. commercial 5. gradual 6. individual 7. actual 8. eventual

Task 5 1. flexible 10. incredible 11. impossible 12. probability 13. responsibility 14. productivity 15. modify
16. diversify

Task 6 1. obvious 2. ambitious 3. industrious 4. spontaneous 5. simultaneous 6. instantaneous 7. ambiguous
8. superfluous 9. trainee 10. employee 11. guarantee 12. interviewee

3.2 Articulation 2

Task 1 2. sales volume 3. production team 4. price war 5. parent company 6. board meeting 7. profit margin
8. trade barriers 9. marketing mix 10. consumer spending 11. market share 12. market forces 13. fix prices
14. process orders 15. promote sales 16. reduce costs 17. train staff 18. fund research 19. agree terms 20. offset costs 21. market products 22. give discounts 23. quote figures 24. talk money 25. net profit 26. corporate client
27. multinational company 28. fixed assets 29. technological lead 30. economic outlook 31. annual report
32. managerial skills 33. free trade 34. low profitability 35. scientific research 36. cultural awareness

Task 2 1. research and <u>development</u> 2. stocks and <u>shares</u> 3. time and <u>motion</u> 4. training and <u>development</u>
5. aims and <u>objectives</u> 6. trial and <u>error</u> 7. pros and <u>cons</u> 8. ups and <u>downs</u> 9. ins and <u>outs</u>

Task 3 1. US<u>A</u> 2. U<u>N</u> 3. E<u>U</u> 4. CI<u>A</u> 5. FB<u>I</u> 6. IB<u>M</u> 7. IM<u>F</u> 8. CN<u>N</u> 9. BBC 10. UA<u>E</u> 11. GDP 12. R&D

Task 4 1. increase <u>profit</u> margins 2. employ temporary <u>staff</u> 3. enter foreign <u>markets</u> 4. create new <u>opportunities</u>
5. annual <u>sales</u> figures 6. competitive <u>performance</u> record 7. <u>stock</u> market report 8. high-technology <u>industry</u>
9. long-term <u>goals</u> 10. far-reaching <u>consequences</u>

3.3 Chunking 1

Task 1 Suggested Version: There's one area of business / where the best / will always find a job. / And it's so vital to the economy / that its success / is almost guaranteed. / The true professional in this field / has nothing to fear from technology / or the changing marketplace. / In fact, / they can virtually name their own salary, / as they provide an essential service, / without which / most companies / would simply go out of business. / I'm talking, / of course, / about selling. /

Task 2 Suggested Version: If the free market is so efficient, / why, / in terms of its environmental consequences, / is the global economy so inefficient? / The answer is simple. / Marketers are brilliant at setting prices, / but quite incapable / of taking costs into account. / Today / we have a free market / that does irreparable damage to the environment / because it does not reflect / the true costs / of products and services. / The proposals I will be outlining this afternoon / all concern, / in one way or another, / this fundamental flaw / in the free market system.

3.4 Chunking 2

Task 2 Suggested Version 1: A company / is, / in many ways, / a political organism. / But, / as far as I'm concerned, / there's no place / for political agendas / in any company I'm running. / So / to prevent / political / and territorial battles / breaking out, / I have two / golden / rules. / First, / I make sure / that departments interfere / as little as possible / in each other's business. / And, second, / I keep everyone / fully informed / of developments / in all departments. / There are no secrets. / Once you have secrets / in an organization, / you start getting into company politics. /

Suggested Version 2: A company is, / in many ways, / a political organism. / But, as far as I'm concerned, / there's no place for political agendas / in any company I'm running. / So to prevent / political and territorial battles breaking out, / I have two golden rules. / First, I make sure / that departments interfere as little as possible / in each other's business. / And, second, / I keep everyone fully informed / of developments in all departments. / There are no secrets. / Once you have secrets in an organization, / you start getting into company politics. /

3.5 Chunking 3

Task 1 1b. We attended the conference / on trade tariffs in Japan. 2a. Those who sold their shares immediately / made a profit. 2b. Those who sold their shares / immediately made a profit. 3a. The Germans / who backed the proposal / are pleased with the results. 3b. The Germans who backed the proposal / are pleased with the results. 4a. It's time to withdraw the economy models / which aren't selling. 4b. It's time to withdraw / the economy models which aren't selling.

3.6 Stress

1b. The British will <u>never</u> agree to that. Not in a million years. 2a. <u>Sales</u> are up on last year. But profits have hardly moved at all. 2b. Sales are are up on <u>last</u> year. But then that was a particularly bad year. 3a. We may not get the <u>whole</u> contract. But we'll get a good part of it. 3b. <u>We</u> may not get the whole contract, but someone will. 4a. The <u>market</u> may be growing. But our market share certainly isn't. 4b. The market <u>may</u> be growing. But, then again, it might just be a seasonal fluctuation. 5a._<u>I</u> think we're making progress. But some of you may not agree with me. 5b. I <u>think</u> we're making progress. But it's very difficult to say at this stage. 6a. We haven't seen a <u>massive</u> improvement yet. But 2% is quite encouraging. 6b. We haven't seen a massive improvement <u>yet.</u> But we soon will. 7a. Our products sell in <u>Sweden</u>. But they don't sell in Denmark. 7b. Our products <u>sell</u> in Sweden. But they don't sell enough. 8a. It's <u>hard</u> to break into Korea. But not impossible. 8b. It's hard to break into <u>Korea</u>. But harder still to break into Japan. 9a. There are <u>three</u> points I'd like to make. And all three concern senior management. 9b. There are three points <u>I'd</u> like to make. And then I'll hand you over to David.

3.7 Pacing

Task 1 2. a 3. b 4. c 5. a 6. c

Task 2 Suggested Versions: 1. This has never ever happened before. 2. We keep getting the same result – time after time after time. 3. Believe me, we will win the business – it's only a matter of time. 4. If we'd known then what we know now, we'd never have gone ahead. 5. We were number one then. We're number one now. And we always will be.

4.1 Emphasis 1

2. It **is** difficult to see what the underlying trend is. 3. We **will** get the price we want in the end. 4. $10,000 is **not** worth worrying about. 5. We do **not** see any need for further injections of cash. 6. They **did** promise to have the feasibility study completed by now. 7. Have we or have we **not** enjoyed ten years of sustained growth? 8. I **would** just like to say that we will be reviewing the whole situation in six months time. 9. Look, we **have** been through all this before and we are not going through it all again. 10. We offered them an apology and we **had** hoped that would be the end of the matter. 11. We **were** hoping to reach an agreement by May, but that is not going to be possible now. 12. We **do** appreciate the need to take risks, but we **do** have our shareholders to think of too. 13.We **do** understand the pressure you are all working under, but we have got a business to run, you know. 14. We were **not** aware of any change in the bank's circumstances, but I **do** think we **should** have been informed. 15. The loss of 4% of our business to the Austrians is **not** a serious matter, but it **is** serious enough to demand our attention this morning – so, what is going on?

4.2 Emphasis 2

2. The whole project is badly underfunded. 3. It's pretty obvious that we made a terrible mistake. 4. It actually works out much cheaper to take on casual workers. 5. I'm fully aware that it's been a total disaster from start to finish. 6. I'm one hundred percent certain that we're in a significantly better position now. 7. There's absolutely no hope at all of reaching our targets by the end of phase two. 8. There's been a dramatic decrease in demand, and yet sales are well up on last year. 9. We really shouldn't be neglecting such a highly lucrative market. 10. There's absolutely no chance whatsoever of making real progress. 11. It's just going to be far too expensive to re-equip the entire factory. 12. It's just so difficult to know whether the figures are actually going to improve. 13. We really can't be expected to manage on such a tiny budget. It's just ridiculous. 14. It's actually far too late to do anything about it at all.

4.3 Emphasis 3

2. a, 1   3. d, 3   4. b, 4   5. h, 2   6. g, 1   7. e, 4   8. f, 3   9. k, 2   10. l, 3   11. i, 4   12. j, 1

4.4 Emphasis 4

Task 2 1. It's theee business opportunity of the year. 2. The Jaguar isn't just an executive car – it's theee executive car. 3. It's theee single biggest market as far as the telecommunications industry is concerned. 4. When it comes to fast-moving consumer goods, the Koreans are theee people to talk to. 5. A joint venture may not turn out to be theee solution, but it's the best solution for now. 6. The fact is, we're not just experts - we're theee experts in the field. 7. Floating the company on the stock exchange is probably theee best thing we ever did.

4.5 Emphasis 5

Task 1 Adding: 1, 4, 5, 7, 8 Emphasizing: 2, 3, 6, 9, 10   **Task 2** 1. c 2. d 3. b 4. a

Task 3 1. difficult 2. critical 3. risky 4. impractical 5. important 6. vital 7. dangerous 8. essential 9. significant 10. inconvenient 11. problematic 12. crucial

4.6 Focusing

Task 1 1. What I'm going to do is talk about motivation. 2. What I'd like to do is move on to the question of cashflow. 3. What I've tried to do is put our recent difficulties into some kind of perspective. 4. What we have to do is consider what the start-up costs might be. 5. What I'll be doing is making a case for getting in a team of specialists. 6. What I'd like you to do is ask yourselves a simple question. 7. What we're aiming to do is be back in the black by the end of this accounting period. 8. What I'm going to be doing is looking at the arguments against networking. 9. What we did was find out how pirate copies of the CD were getting into stores. 10. What I want to know is how long it'll be before we start seeing a profit.

Task 2　1. don't want　2. we haven't done　3. What we aren't　4. What I'm not prepared　5. What we are trying
6. What does matter is how

4.7　Softening 1

2. I sometimes think we're just a little too price-conscious.　3. All in all, I'd say we'll just about manage to break even.　4. It's basically a good idea, but it's almost certain to meet opposition.　5. I'm fairly pleased with our performance and, all in all, it's been quite a good year.　6. In Northern Europe the response to our mailshots has generally been rather poor and I think that's partly the result of deciding to target only large firms.　7. We've probably done a bit better than we expected this year, although I have to say that net profits are still rather low.
8. We had a few minor hiccups during the launch and it's been pretty hard work getting the advertising right, but everything's more or less OK now.　9. The procedure is virtually foolproof.　If we do occasionally make slight errors of judgement, they're usually fairly easy to put right.

4.8　Softening 2

1. encouraging, admit　2. happy, true　3. easy, need　4. growing, grant　5. success, sorry　6. help, sure　7. boom, things　8. make, afraid　9. well, point　10. better, pretend

4.9　Repetition 1

Task 1　1. It's obviously very, very tempting to close down plants which aren't breaking even.　2. The short-term benefits are obvious, but it's much, much more difficult to say what the long-term benefits might be.　3. It's way, way too soon to say just how successful this new initiative has been.　4. There are many, many reasons why it's very, very important to get the go-ahead from Brussels.　5. Their demands are absolutely ridiculous and we'll never, never agree to them.　6. One thing you can be totally sure of: there'll always, always be a market for quality.
Task 2　1. I'm happy to report that our presence in Singapore is getting stronger and stronger.　2. As the competition gets tougher and tougher, we just get better and better.　3. As the smaller companies go to the wall, fewer and fewer players remain in the market.　4. It's getting harder and harder to make money and easier and easier to lose it.　5. These days more and more firms are turning to freelance consultants.　6. Over the next ten years management positions are going to become less and less secure.　7. As new technology moves faster and faster, data protection becomes more and more of a problem.　8. More and more people are fighting over fewer and fewer jobs for less and less money.

4.10　Repetition 2

Task 1　2. Profits are down ... Profits are down because costs have risen.　3. The market is flat ... The market is flat because we're still in recession.　4. The figures are disappointing ... The figures are disappointing because we were expecting too much.　5. We need new product ... We need new product because we are falling behind the competition.　6. We know it won't work ... We know it won't work because we've done it before.　7. Price is everything ... Price is everything because the market is saturated.　8.The prospects are good ... The prospects are good because we've established a firm foothold in Europe.
Task 2　1. The time to act is now ... The time to act is now while the opportunities are still there.　2. The results have been very encouraging ... The results have been very encouraging in spite of difficult circumstances.　3. It's time to change strategy ... It's time to change strategy before it's too late.　4. It's easy to take risks ... It's easy to take risks when you're not risking your own money!

4.11　Repetition 3

1. No-one, no-one　2. Nothing, nothing　3. Nowhere, nowhere　4. No, not one　5. Every, every one　6. never, never　7. always, always　8. ever, ever　9. no, none at all　10. everyone, everyone

5.1　Rhetorical Questions 1

1. how + do　2. what + waiting　3. where + go　4. how soon + seeing　5. how long + making
6. what sort + looking　7. where + did　8. how come + feeling　9. how much + is　10. what + attribute　11. what + take　12. how + working

5.2　Rhetorical Questions 2

Task 1　1. g　2. c　3. a　4. f　5. d　6. b　7. h　8. e; a. all of them　b. b, c, e, f, h

5.3 Rhetorical Questions 3

1. problem, problem 2. result, result 3. objective, objective 4. answer, answer 5. point, point 6. idea, idea 7. prospects, prospects 8. chances, chances 9. advantages, advantages

5.4 Dramatic Contrasts 1

1. j 2. d 3. g 4. b 5. i 6. h 7. c 8. f 9. e 10. a

5.5 Dramatic Contrasts 2

1. can do for your country 2. is a failure 3. you lose yours 4. it has 5. of it again 6. of the past 7. something I hate 8. say something 9. what you get 10. wife to his success 11. lose them all 12. on the golf-course

5.6 Tripling 1

Task 2 1. e 2. c 3. b 4. a 5. d   **Task 3** 1. e 2. a 3. b 4. c 5. d

5.7 Tripling 2

Task 1 2. What's the answer? Simple. Work harder, work faster, work smarter. 3. Where are the best opportunities? It's obvious. In Germany, in Japan, in Brazil. 4. Can we improve performance? Yes. In terms of output, in terms of turnover, in terms of profit margin. 5. What would cuts mean at this stage? Disaster! No new plant, no new product, no new ideas! 6. Change the system and what do you get? Problems. Problems with workers, problems with distributors, problems with customers.

Task 2 1. How can we beat the Koreans? I'll tell you. On reliability, on quality, on price. That's how. 2. Does comparative advertising get results? Of course it does. Ask IBM. Ask Apple. Ask Pepsi. They'll tell you. 3. Can market leadership be achieved in computers? Sure it can. Look at Tom Watson. Look at John Sculley. Look at Bill Gates. They did it. 4. How are we doing? Better than ever. The customers like us. The shareholders like us. The banks like us! Need I say more?

5.8 Tripling 3

Task 1 1. "**Never** / in the **field** of human **conflict** / was **so much** / owed by **so many** / to **so few**." 2. "You can fool **all** the people / **some** of the time / and **some** of the people / **all** the time, / but you cannot fool **all** the people / **all** the time." 3. "What is a **committee**? / A **group** of the **unwilling**, / picked from the **unfit** / to do the **unnecessary**." 4. "**People** can be divided into **three** groups: / those who **make** things happen, / those who **watch** things happen / and those who ask '**What happened?**'" 5. "**This** is **not** the **end**. / It is not **even** the **beginning** of the **end**. / But it **is**, / perhaps, / the **end** of the **beginning**." 6. "**Coming** together is a **beginning**; / **keeping** together is **progress**; / **working** together is **success**." 7. "**Organizations** don't have new **ideas**. / **Teams** don't have new **ideas**. / **Individuals** have new **ideas**. / **That's** why **you** come **first**." 8. "There are **three** types of **lies:** / **lies**, / **damned lies** / and **statistics**." 9. "The **other** man's word is an **opinion**; / **yours** is the **truth**; / and your **boss's** is **law**." 10. "Most **presentations** / have **three** basic **stages:** / **tell** them what you're going to **tell** them; / **tell** them; / **tell** them what you **told** them." 11. The **old** / **believe** everything; / the **middle-aged** / **suspect** everything; / the **young** / **know** everything." 12. "All the things / I **really** like to do / are either **immoral, / illegal, /** or **fattening**."

Task 2 1. succeed – try – try 2. sex – money – power 3. Everyone – fool – computer 4. Today – tomorrow – yesterday 5. Nothing – Everything – anything 6. Lead – follow – get

5.9 Machine-Gunning

Task 2 1. c 2. a 3. b

5.10 Build-ups

1. dividends, costs; b 2. requirements, price, impression; c 3. access, road, grant; d 4. process, production, channels, stores; e 5. trip, business, exchange, agent; a

5.11 Knock-downs

1. well-established, quality, service, priced; b 2. access, confidential, programs, system; d 3. persuade, management, pursuing, backing, ground; a 4. model, storm, reviews, trade, competition; c

5.12 Simplification

2. ~~If you~~ pack in too many ~~product~~ features, ~~naturally~~ your prices go up and ~~eventually~~ you lose customers.

3. ~~The~~ question ~~is,~~ how ~~are we going~~ to break even? ~~And the~~ answer, ~~I think, is~~ to focus ~~our attention~~ on efficiency. 4. ~~What about~~ diversification? ~~Is it~~ a good idea? Sure, ~~it is.~~ But ~~isn't it a bit~~ too late? Yes, ~~I'm sorry to~~

~~say, it~~ probably ~~is~~. 5. In 1981 ~~we were making~~ huge losses. This year ~~we've become~~ the market leader. How ~~do you explain that? It's really very~~ simple. We worked ~~very hard~~ for it. 6. ~~So,~~ we've massively overspent. ~~The~~ answer ~~is to cut back now. But just~~ how ~~are we going to do this?~~ ~~Well, that's~~ easy. ~~There will have to be~~ a wage freeze. 7. ~~So, what about~~ the merger? ~~Do we agree to~~ go ahead ~~with it~~ now? Or ~~do we decide to~~ wait ~~until our position is clearer~~? Obviously, ~~for the time being~~ we ~~should~~ wait. 8. ~~Basically, we're having~~ three problems. ~~Number~~ one, ~~we don't have the~~ money ~~we need~~. ~~Number~~ two, ~~we have~~ insufficient experience ~~in this field~~. And ~~number~~ three, ~~there's far~~ too much competition ~~around~~. 9. ~~The point is,~~ big companies are out ~~of fashion these days~~. And ~~it's the~~ small companies ~~who~~ are in. ~~To give you an example,~~ look at IBM. Once ~~they were~~ at the top ~~of the computer industry~~. Now ~~its~~ more of a struggle.

5.13 Creating Rapport 1

Task 1 1. I'm sure the implications of the proposed merger are clear to all of us. 2. I want us all to be thinking of ways in which we can maximize sales. 3. We're aiming to turn the losses we've been making into profits within eighteen months. 4. We all know from our own experience how difficult it is to re-establish ourselves in an overseas market. 5. I think we all need to ask ourselves how long we can go on exceeding our budget.

Task 2 1. We have to reorganize if we're to survive, don't we? And that won't be easy, will it? 2. It isn't really a question of marketing, is it? It's more a question of product management, isn't it? 3. Clearly, the results are better than we expected, aren't they? But then we weren't expecting much, were we? 4. We've all talked about this before, haven't we? And I don't think we've ever reached a proper decision, have we? Still, that's not surprising, given the circumstances, is it? 5. We can't really blame our poor performance on the local economy, can we? Because that's supposed to be improving, isn't it? But what we can do is look at global trends, can't we?

Task 3 1. Isn't it about time we took a fresh look at packaging? 2. Didn't I tell you we'd exceed our targets? Don't we always? 3. Aren't we fortunate to have weathered the recession as well as we have? 4. Don't we want shorter hours? Don't we want better conditions? Don't we want higher pay? 5. Isn't there a need for more teamwork? Isn't this something we should be looking at?

5.14 Creating Rapport 2

Task 2 1. OK, so 2. well 3. you know 4. you see 5. actually 6. as a matter of fact 7. so / then 8. OK? 9. now

5.15 Creating Rapport 3

Task 1 1. e 2. d 3. f 4. a 5. b 6. c   **Task 2** 1. f 2. d 3. e 4. b 5. c 6. a

6.1 Business Terms 1

Task 2 fairly: buoyant, flat, sluggish, static, brisk, slow, slack, strong, sound, stable, weak, considerable, negligible, reasonable, unsatisfactory, poor, competitive. **virtually:** flat, saturated, stable, disastrous, negligible, unbeatable. **extremely:** buoyant, flat, saturated, sluggish, slow, slack, strong, sound, stable, weak, encouraging, disappointing, unsatisfactory, poor, competitive. **absolutely:** flat, saturated, booming, static, thriving, sound, stable, excellent, disastrous, enormous, negligible, first-class, unbeatable.

6.2 Business Terms 2

Task 2 very: bright, promising, uncertain, bleak, generous, attractive, fair, good, limited, minor, substantial, successful, productive, dramatic, rapid, steady, gradual, modest, considerable, uncompetitive, unprofitable. **relatively:** bright, promising, uncertain, bleak, generous, attractive, good, limited, negligible, minor, substantial, successful, productive, inconclusive, rapid, steady, insignificant, modest, unprofitable, unmarketable. **highly:** promising, uncertain, attractive, limited, substantial, successful, productive, dramatic. **totally:** uncertain, bleak, unacceptable, non-existent, negligible, enormous, successful, inconclusive, fruitless, insignificant, prohibitive, unbeatable, uncompetitive, unprofitable, unmarketable.

6.3 Business Terms 3

1. place, receive, confirm, process, dispatch 2. set up, expand, put...on the market, sell off, buy back 3. instigate, launch, work on, jeopardize, axe 4. headhunt, recruit, train, promote, dismiss 5. come up with, put forward, consider, accept, implement

6.4 Business Terms 4

1. target, break into, be forced out of, re-enter, take over 2. enter into, conduct, break off, resume, complete

3. set, raise, receive complaints about, re-think, cut 4. negotiate, draw up, renew, breach, terminate 5. develop, manufacture, launch, distribute, withdraw

6.5 Business Terms 5

1. suspect, identify, clarify, tackle, solve 2. forecast, suffer, announce, write off, recover from 3. devise, produce, run, update, re-run 4. believe in, put money into, carry out, cut back on, abandon 5. identify, take on, undercut, outsell, destroy

6.6 Business Terms 6

2. prices 3. an opportunity 4. a product 5. a budget 6. matters 7. customers 8. costs 9. restrictions 10. the competition 11. an offer 12. a strategy 13. a deadline 14. capital 15. a decision 16. staff 17. production 18. a reputation

6.7 Formality 1

2. a, 4   3. d, 3   4. b, 1   5. f, 3   6. h, 1   7. e, 2   8. g, 4   9. l, 2   10. k, 4   11. j, 1   12. i, 3   13. o, 2   14. p, 1   15. m, 4   16. n, 3   17. t, 1   18. s, 2   19. q, 4   20. r, 3

6.8 Formality 2

1. Everybody knows that the Internet is the information channel of the future. 2. They've proved that direct mailing gets a less than 1% response rate. 3. They're suggesting that so-called smart drugs can actually increase intelligence. 4. Almost everyone agrees that the number of new cases of AIDS is falling. 5. A lot of us believe that Thailand and Malaysia will continue to outgrow Taiwan. 6. We don't know whether a mile-high building is technically possible. 7. A lot of people don't realize that more people die of tuberculosis every year than were killed in both world wars. 8. People often make the mistake of thinking that Total Quality originated in Japan. 9. We can't be sure whether we can achieve such an ambitious project in two years. 10. We don't expect anyone to find a cure for the common cold.

6.9 Useful Expressions 1

Part 1 a. take b. taken c. give d. doing e. made f. make

Part 2 a. take b. give c. doing d. make e. takes f. made g. take

Part 3 a. make b. take c. make d. make e. taking f. making g. do h. taking i. making j. making

Part 4 a. making b. making c. taken d. give e. make f. done g. take h. done i. give j. give k. done

6.10 Useful Expressions 2

Part 1 a. get b. getting c. got d. getting e. got f. get g. got h. get

Part 2 a. taking b. take c. taken d. take e. take f. take g. take h. taking

Part 3 a. going b. go c. gone d. goes e. go f. going g. go

6.11 Useful Expressions 3

Task 1 1. e, In 2. d, As 3. a, At 4. b, On 5. c, Up   **Task 2** 1. b, Up 2. c, On 3. e, In 4. a, As 5. d, At
Task 3 1. c, In 2. d, As 3. e, Up 4. b, On 5. a, At

6.12 Useful Expressions 4

Task 1 1. d, On 2. a, As 3. e, In 4. b, Under 5. c, At **Task 2** 1. b, As 2. e, At 3. d, Under 4. a, On 5. c, In
Task 3 1. c, In 2. e, As 3. b, On 4. a, At 5. d, Under

7.1 Clarification 1

Task 1 1. missed + say 2. catch + repeat 3. follow + run 4. see + explain

Task 3 1. Sorry, thinking of what? 2. Sorry, exporting to where? 3. Sorry, the best person is who? 4. Sorry, the market leaders are who? 5. Sorry, we must reach our preliminary target by when? 6. Sorry, the main problem is going to be what? 7. Sorry, advertising has cost us well over how much? 8. Sorry, the answer is what? 9. Sorry, Brazil is very different from where? 10. Sorry, we need to be putting money into what? 11. Sorry, you should know the results by when? 12. Sorry, you've been forced to cut prices by how much? 13. Sorry, it might take how long to finalize the details? 14. Sorry, there are more than how many similar products on the market?

7.2 Clarification 2

Suggested Clarification Questions and Answers: 1. Sorry, looking at what in Eastern Europe? The economic situation. 2. Sorry, projections to when? To 2010. 3. Sorry, over the next how long? Over the next five years.

4. Sorry, the Czech Republic's credit rating is what? Triple-B. 5. Sorry, they paid off their IMF debt when? In 1994. 6. Sorry, the debt stood at what? 470 million. 7. Sorry, four or five percent what? Growth. 8. Sorry, the problem in Poland is what? Inflation. 9. Sorry, kept below how much? 20%. 10. Sorry, who were economic reformists? The Hungarians. 11. Sorry, Hungary's growth rate is rather what? Rather disappointing. 12. Sorry, the amount of foreign what? Investment. 13. Sorry, how much was invested? 18 billion dollars. 14. Sorry, almost how much? Almost a third.

7.3 Clarification 3

1. talking 2. describing 3. dealing 4. summing up 5. showing 6. telling

1. quoted 2. commented 3. made 4. said 5. spoke 6. referred

1. tell 2. say 3. explain 4. be 5. elaborate 6. run

7.4 Dealing with Questions 1

Good: 6, 11, 14 Difficult: 3, 4, 7, 9, 10, 15 Unnecessary: 5, 8, 12 Irrelevant: 1, 2, 13

7.5 Dealing with Questions 2

Suggested Questions and Answers: **Q1: You mentioned 1989. Do you have precise profit and loss figures for that year?** A1: I'm afraid I don't have that information with me. **Q2: One question. How do we plan to regain market leadership?** A2: That's a very good question. **Q3: I'd be interested to know how our improved performance will be reflected in salaries.** A3: To be honest, I think that raises a rather different issue. **Q4: How, in fact, did we manage to win back business from the Japanese?** A4: Well, as I said, by introducing total quality throughout the company. **Q5: You talked about quality, but you didn't talk about product diversification. Why not?** A5: I'm afraid I don't see the connection. **Q6: Why do you think we were so slow to respond to the competition in the 80's?** A6: Good point. What do you think? **Q7: How does our current position compare with the situation in the early 80's?** A7: I think I answered that earlier. We've regained most of the market share we lost. **Q8: What nobody's said so far is that the market itself is declining. Doesn't this offset most of the gains we've made?** A8: I'm glad you asked that. I'll be dealing with current market trends later. **Q9: You've said a lot about market share, but you haven't told us what it's cost us. We must have eaten into our reserves. I'd like to see the cashflow statement.** A9: I'm afraid I don't have that information with me. Can I get back to you on that?

7.6 Dealing with Questions 3

Exchange 1 1, 5, 4, 3, 2 **Exchange 2** 1, 4, 2, 5, 3 **Exchange 3** 1, 3, 5, 4, 2 **Exchange 4** 1, 3, 5, 2, 4 **Exchange 5** 1, 4, 2, 5, 3

7.7 Dealing with Questions 4

Exchange 1 1, 5, 2, 4, 3 **Exchange 2** 1, 5, 3, 2, 4 **Exchange 3** 1, 4, 3, 2, 5 **Exchange 4** 1, 4, 5, 3, 2 **Exchange 5** 1, 5, 4, 2, 3

7.8 Dealing with Questions 5

Exchange 1 1, 4, 3, 2, 5 **Exchange 2** 1, 4, 3, 2, 5 **Exchange 3** 1, 3, 2, 5, 4 **Exchange 4** 1, 4, 5, 2, 3 **Exchange 5** 1, 5, 4, 3, 2

7.9 Dealing with Questions 6

Exchange 1 1. Not yet. 2. True. 3. To some extent. 4. Hopefully not. **Exchange 2** 1. Not quite. 2. Not necessarily. 3. Yes, I know. 4. Not as a rule. **Exchange 3** 1. Not at all. 2. Not really. 3. Granted. 4. Not entirely. **Exchange 4** 1. Yes and no. 2. It depends. 3. Not if we can help it. 4. On the whole, yes.